Staffordshire Library and Information Service

Please return or renew or by the last date shown

If not required by other readers, this item may be renewed
in person, by post or telephone, online or by email.
To renew, either the book or ticket are required

24 Hour Renewal Line
0845 33 00 740

 Staffordshire
County Council

THE STORY OF
ROMAN BATH

PATRICIA SOUTHERN

AMBERLEY

Unless otherwise stated all colour photographs of the Roman Baths are © Bath & North East Somerset Council. Photographer, Jonathan Reeve.

First published 2012
Amberley Publishing
The Hill, Stroud
Gloucestershire, GL5 4EP

www.amberleybooks.com

British Library Cataloguing in Publication Data.
A catalogue record for this book is available from the British Library.

ISBN 978 1 4456 1090 0

Typeset in 11pt on 17.6pt Sabon.
Typesetting and Origination by Amberley Publishing.
Printed in the UK.

CONTENTS

PREFACE

It is probably safe to say that Aquae Sulis was unique in Roman Britain, because it did not slot conveniently into any of the categories of Romano-British civil settlements, and no other site could boast such an impressive array of spa baths, conventional baths, temple precinct and healing springs. Similarly, modern Bath, a UNESCO World Heritage Site, is unique among the many Roman remains that have been explored in Britain. No other Roman classical temple in Britain is so well known as the temple of Sulis Minerva, where enough sections have been found of the temple pediment and of the columns that supported it to be able to reconstruct its appearance and size. The temple of Claudius in Colchester was probably more important and much more elaborate, but the Normans used whatever was left of it in the eleventh century as the foundation for their huge castle, ensuring that nothing much remained of it for archaeologists to explore. Fortunately for Bath, the Normans did not build a castle on top of the Roman temple. By the time of the conquest by William I, not much of Roman Bath was known, because the hot springs bubbling up more or less undisturbed for the past five or six centuries had buried the Roman town under a thick layer of mud. When the King's Bath was built around AD 1100 and named after Henry I, there was no sign whatsoever that the baths were being erected on top of the sacred spring with its enclosing superstructure, and no-one suspected that the temple of Sulis Minerva lay nearby. During the medieval era it was known that Bath had been a Roman settlement, because many inscribed stones had been used in its walls, but it was not until the eighteenth century when new buildings were being erected that more and stronger evidence was found to show that there had been a temple in the town dedicated to Sulis Minerva, who is attested on several inscriptions.

Anyone trying to write about Roman Bath has to acknowledge and admire the work of Professor Barry Cunliffe and the Bath Excavation Committee formed in the 1960s and then superseded by the Bath Archaeological Trust. The City Council and the Museums Service have always entertained an enlightened attitude to the archaeological investigations and the presentation of the remains and the finds, updating the displays and the guidebooks when such revisions are deemed necessary by further discoveries. There is still much to be learned about Roman Bath, so hopefully new books will always be appearing, which provides a good enough excuse for this one. As well as summarising the archaeology that is exhaustively covered by Professor Cunliffe's books, I have tried to include information about Roman Britain in general so it can be seen how the town fitted into the context of events and trends of the province of Britannia, and sometimes in the Empire, at various stages in the history of Aquae Sulis.

Patricia Southern
Northumberland
2012

I

BATH BEFORE THE ROMANS

The water that bubbles up through the three hot springs of Bath is very old. This is not just because the site was known to the prehistoric people of the area and then developed much later by the Romans, but because it can take several thousand years for the rain that falls on the Mendips to sink down through the rock towards the centre of the earth, re-emerging with its acquired heat and minerals to provide the spa town with its famous baths.

On the way down through the earth's crust the rainwater approaches but does not reach the hot molten core, absorbing more and more heat as it descends. At a depth of about 3,000 to 4,000 metres, at a temperature somewhere between 60 degrees centigrade and 90 degrees centigrade the water reverses its course and starts to come back to the surface, losing some of its heat but none of its minerals and salts as it gushes from the earth at the rate of 250,000 gallons a day. The hot spring water emerges at one point of origin deep within the earth, but before it finds its way out at ground level it splits up via three different outlets, all quite close together.

The temperature of the water varies a little between the three springs. The appropriately named Hot Bath is the warmest at 49 degrees centigrade (120 degrees Fahrenheit), and the Cross Bath spring the coolest at 40 degrees centigrade (114 degrees

Fahrenheit). The King's Bath spring provides the strongest and most prolific flow of water, at a temperature of 46 degrees centigrade (117 degrees Fahrenheit). The orange colour that stains the baths derives from the iron content of the water, and besides the iron there are over forty other minerals, the most prevalent being calcium sulphate, sodium sulphate, and magnesium chloride, with lesser proportions of strontium sulphate, potassium sulphate, calcium carbonate, and sodium chloride. There are also traces of lithium, bromine and silica.

The original Roman bathing complex of the first century AD was continually enlarged and developed, covering a large area of the town. When the medieval and modern baths were built there was little if any knowledge of the Roman structures that lay beneath them, though it was clear from the remains of sculptures and inscribed stones that the Romans had occupied the place. The King's Bath is said to have been named in the twelfth century after King Henry I, and the name was retained through the following centuries. When John Leland visited Bath in the reign of Henry VIII he described the King's Bath, the Cross Bath and the Hot Bath, and in 1610 John Speed included a drawing of the King's Bath in his map of Somerset, showing it just as Leland described it, enclosed within a rectangular, walled precinct, with an inner arcade all round the bath providing niches for the bathers to stand in. The Pump Room was an additional building of the eighteenth century, originally built in 1706, by Richard Nash, better known as Beau Nash. Nearly a century later the Pump Room was rebuilt in its present form by John Palmer. It was re-opened to the public in 1799. The names of the bathing establishments became more elaborate as time went on. A nineteenth-century guidebook lists the King's Bath, the Queen's Bath, the Old Royal Baths, where the Hot Springs emerged, and the New Royal Baths. These were open on weekdays from 7 a.m. till 7 p.m. The current names have reverted to the usage of medieval times: the King's Bath, the Cross Bath and the Hot Bath. The Great Bath is the main Roman one.

The site where the Roman town of Bath was to be established is surrounded on the west, south and east sides by a loop of the River Avon, with open, hilly land to the north and north-west. The spring of the King's Bath emerges between two small hills, while the waters of the Hot Bath and the Cross Bath rise a short distance away on the hill to the west of the King's Bath. No-one knows what the ancient Britons called the place, but when the Romans arrived and named it Aquae Sulis, the Waters of Sulis, they presumably preserved the name of the Iron Age British deity who was associated with the springs. From the very earliest times onwards, the ancient Britons could not have failed to notice the site, where the hot water bursting from the three springs would have created a misty environment all around the surrounding marshy area, and the land and vegetation would have been stained with the orange colour left by the iron content of the water.

Whether or not the Britons used the springs for their healing qualities is not known for certain, but it is very likely that they did. The whole area surrounding the springs would probably have been revered as a mysterious, magical place and would very probably have been attributed to some deity. Mystery, magic, superstition and religion were usually all inseparably fused together in ancient societies. If the site was imbued with religious significance, the Britons may have worshipped there, possibly as far back as the Palaeolithic era or the Old Stone Age.

The terminology applied to prehistoric periods is entirely artificial but serves to distinguish the extremely long timespans by dividing them into more manageable units. Before the invention of written records, there is no knowledge of personal names or place names. Even the languages that prehistoric people spoke are completely unknown. Since it is not possible for archaeologists to divide up prehistory according to political or social developments, instead they define the tools and weapons that people used. The Bronze Age and the Iron Age speak for themselves, but stone tools were used for a considerably longer period than metal tools, becoming more sophisticated as time went on. Archaeologists distinguish between the different Stone Age eras by using terms derived from ancient Greek. Palaeolithic derives from two Greek roots, the *palaeo* element meaning old and the *lithic* element deriving from the word for stone. Similarly Mesolithic means the Middle Stone Age, when a detectable change can be seen in the type of tools and weapons that the people left behind them. These tools are more sophisticated than those of the Palaeolithic era, but not yet identifiable with the stone tools of the Neolithic, or New Stone Age. These named periods of history are not exactly the same all over Europe and the Near East, because the introduction of new ways of life in one country sometimes pre-dated their development in other countries by hundreds of years. The Neolithic era, when ancient people started to grow crops and to domesticate animals, began in the Near East around 10,000 BC, but did not begin in Britain until around 4500 BC.

The Mesolithic and Neolithic Eras

In the area around Bath there are traces of human activity during the Mesolithic and Neolithic periods, but no firm evidence that any of these people settled in the vicinity of the springs or even utilised them in any way. This is largely because they did not leave behind them any easily detectable traces. Their weapons and tools would be carried with them, and their dwellings were made of wood, leaving only slightly different-coloured earth where the post-holes had been situated. The association of prehistoric people with the springs is therefore reliant upon generalisations from what is known of their way of life, enhanced by large amounts of speculation. But the hot springs are such a noticeable feature of the landscape that it is difficult to imagine that the prehistoric people ignored or avoided them altogether.

The change from the Palaeolithic to the Mesolithic period is discernible in Britain from about 8000 BC, but the dates for the end of one way of life and its substitution by another cannot be established with such abrupt certainty, because the change was very gradual and did not happen at exactly the same time all over the country. Mesolithic people were hunter-gatherers, living off the land by hunting animals and gathering wild food. Meat was probably the main constituent of their diet. These people used the land and all its products, but did not farm it or grow crops. In the area surrounding Bath the signs of Mesolithic activity are slight, largely because the Mesolithic people were mobile, continually following the animals that they hunted, which provided them with food, skins for clothing and bones to make tools. They also gathered food until it was exhausted and then moved on, although in recent years it has been shown that the hunter-gatherers were not as mobile and rootless as previously thought. They set up base camps to which they returned periodically, but the traces of their dwellings, built of timber and probably thatched, are difficult to discern unless careful excavation techniques are applied. Their houses would have been substantial enough to shelter them adequately for short periods, but in general they were too flimsy to leave definite archaeological traces behind them thousands of years after they were built. The most common finds from Mesolithic sites are flint tools, mostly hand-held scrapers and the tiny flint arrowheads that the people fashioned for hunting and no doubt for fighting each other. These arrowheads are known as microliths, meaning 'small stones', and scatters of such flint tools can identify a place where these people camped.

From such ephemeral signs, it is clear that Mesolithic hunter-gatherers did make camps near the springs where the city of Bath would be established, but that is the limit of knowledge about them. What they did there and how long they stayed on each visit cannot be elucidated without further finds. It is not even known what tribe they came from, if indeed tribes had been formed at that time, nor what language they spoke, nor which deities they worshipped at Bath, nor if they performed religious ceremonies there.

The Neolithic farmers of the New Stone Age succeeded the Mesolithic people, though probably not via an aggressive series of invasions in which Mesolithic hunter-gatherers were eradicated. It is thought that there would have been a gradual process of amalgamation and adoption of new ways of life. For some considerable time, flint tools and weapons were used side by side with the newfangled stone versions, but flint eventually went out of use as the spread of stone tools increased. Flint tools can be honed to form very fine, sharp edges, but one man using a stone axe can probably chop down more trees more quickly than another man wielding flint tools. As time went on the Mesolithic and Neolithic lifestyles merged. This meld of cultures is called acculturation by archaeologists. Between the Mesolithic and the Neolithic, acculturation probably occurred very slowly over many generations, a process that cannot be illustrated in detail. The farmers gradually became more settled and attached to the land, probably combining hunting and gathering with crop growing and animal husbandry. The land around Bath probably saw its first change in status during the Neolithic era. Several settlements are known from the hills around Bath, and although it cannot be said that all the sites that have been discovered were occupied at the same time, there are enough of them, coupled with a large number of artefacts of the Neolithic period, to indicate that many people lived in the area and supported themselves by farming and stock raising. This has important implications for the area of Bath. When the resident population became more sedentary and started to cultivate the land, control of territory and its protection became more important, so the land all around Bath would probably be carved up into smaller units and claimed by the people who made their homes there. In this case, possession of the land, and with it access to the springs, may have been fought over, possibly changing hands sometimes. None of this hypothetical scenario can be verified, and use of the springs by Neolithic people remains conjectural.

The Bronze Age

The changes around Bath during the Bronze Age are just as difficult to discern as those of the Mesolithic and Neolithic. Metal tools and weapons began to appear in Britain in the middle of the third millennium BC, and like the transition between the

Mesolithic and Neolithic eras, the change from use of stone implements to the adoption of metal ones was probably gradual and slow. But the change in society would be more profound in the Bronze Age than in the Stone Age. The manufacture of stone tools required a certain amount of practice and skill, but the creation of metal tools involved true specialists, people with esoteric knowledge and the skill to transform the ore that came from the ground into the desired shapes of daggers, swords, spearheads and various agricultural implements. The occupants of land where metal ores were present automatically possessed an advantage over those who lived in areas with no mineral resources, so they would also possess great bargaining powers with those who needed the ore. On the other hand they would probably have been forced to guard their land more closely and fight to retain these privileges.

In the Bronze Age, the emergence of leaders or kings, and presumably tribal claims to specific territories, is illustrated by the way in which the Bronze Age people treated their dead. The early Neolithic people buried the bones of their dead in communal graves, usually after the flesh had rotted away, or had been deliberately removed. They built stone- or wood-lined chambers to house the bones, left open to the elements for some time. Then they finally closed them and buried the chambers in large, elongated earthen mounds called long barrows. Towards the end of the Neolithic period, cremation of the body and the burial of the bones in sacred places became more common. The Bronze Age people did not bury their dead in communal tombs, nor did they cremate them and place their bones in communal burial places, but they placed certain individuals in graves around which they erected monumental circular mounds of earth, called barrows but clearly distinguishable from the early Neolithic long barrows. The mass of Bronze Age people were not accorded such prestige, so to the modern way of thinking, these burials of individuals accompanied by grave-goods probably signify the last resting places of great men, and sometimes women, who were important in society, if not leaders or kings and queens.

For the history of Bath, by the time of the Bronze Age, there was probably a need for even tighter control of the land and of the hot springs. Even if the use of the waters was accessible to all people on religious grounds, there may have been guardians or possibly religious leaders who co-ordinated ceremonials. This is to go way beyond the evidence, but the alternative, in the absence of evidence for Bronze Age settlement around Bath, is to imagine that the springs were ignored for centuries, their healing properties unknown, and no deity or deities worshipped there.

The Iron Age

The Iron Age people, from roughly the eighth century BC to the first century AD, are more easily detected and studied, because they are closer in time to our own era, which means that the articles they left behind have not had so much time to perish, and because they were less mobile and more settled people than the Mesolithic hunter-gatherers or even the Neolithic farmers, leaving more detectable clues for archaeologists about their way of life. The houses of the Iron Age tribes are more substantial than those of previous eras, and the pottery, weapons and tools, wooden artefacts and textiles associated with settlement sites and burial grounds are better preserved and more abundant. Though there is not as yet any evidence of an Iron Age settlement in the immediate vicinity of the hot springs, the wider area around Bath was populated in the Iron Age. A hill-fort was established on Bathampton Hill, south of the River Avon on the east side of the later town. Another fort was built on the hill top at Little Solsbury to the north of the River Avon. This one was occupied for a few hundred years, and was very strongly defended, suggesting that the period was one of endemic insecurity. At the site of the springs, there are very few signs of occupation, but this simply means that not much has been found there, rather than a categorical denial that anyone actually lived there in the Iron Age.

At some unknown time, the native Britons around Bath developed the cult of the water deity, guardian of the springs, known to the Romans as Sul, or Sulis. No-one knows how far back in time this goddess began to be worshipped. She does not seem to be a Roman import, a goddess who was unknown to the Britons until the first century AD, because otherwise the Romans would probably have dedicated the temple to their goddess Minerva alone, without benefit of a British goddess as her companion.

Sulis may have been a long-established deity, perhaps revered during the Bronze Age, possibly known in some form to the Mesolithic or Neolithic people. She may have been given a series of different names throughout the centuries; perhaps she even changed her gender as different populations honoured a female or a male deity at the springs. The healing attributes of the waters, and hence of the deity, may always have been recognised by the successive generations of people who lived in the area, whatever their name for the god or goddess.

There were several water deities in ancient Britain, of whom

Sulis was only one example. So far there is no evidence that she was worshipped under this name anywhere else. These water deities were worshipped irrespective of whether the water issued from hot springs with healing qualities, or from other water sources without such properties. For the Celtic Iron Age people at least, it is acknowledged that water from springs, pools, lakes and rivers was of the highest religious importance. It is not known whether the Mesolithic and Neolithic people shared the same beliefs. Nothing has so far been discovered in Britain that could be interpreted as Mesolithic offerings to a water deity, but such tributes are known in Scandinavian countries. In the Celtic Iron Age, offerings were made to the gods or goddesses of the waters, as attested by the many objects that were deposited in the water at all these types of places. One famous site is Llyn Cerrig Bach in Anglesey, where the votive deposits contained a large quantity of metalwork, including a gang-chain thought to have been for controlling slaves or a collection of prisoners. The items that were deposited dated from the first century BC, and one of the most important features is that the metalwork was not local to Wales, but originated from other parts of Britain, principally from the south-east. This may mean that a Welsh chieftain traded with other tribes, or exchanged gifts, and then offered some or all of the gifts he received to the water deity. Alternatively the site may have been a well-known religious centre where Iron Age versions of pilgrims came to make offerings. Either solution indicates that the natives of Britain were not gathered in totally isolated local communities, and reinforces the concept that water possessed great significance in their lives. Another site where a water goddess was honoured is the sacred spring at Coventina's Well on Hadrian's Wall in Northumberland, where offerings were still made throughout the Roman period.[1] At Ilkley in Yorkshire, the goddess Verbeia, the spirit of the River Wharfe, was worshipped in Roman times.[2] Presumably she was a native British goddess of the Iron Age who had been given a Romanised name.

It has recently been emphatically pointed out that the term 'Celt' does not denote or define a nation or a nationality, or a people all derived originally from one root, so nowadays the employment of the descriptive term Celtic incurs the risk of ridicule, and demands a qualifying statement. It was the Greeks who labelled the different tribes as Keltoi, recognising certain shared characteristics among divergent peoples, much as the Romans labelled the several tribes from beyond the Danube as Scythians, without distinguishing between the various groups. Tribal names are notoriously unreliable anyway. Even in ancient times, the names did not usually remain immutable for centuries, but new groupings emerged and old ones were subsumed, and the names changed with them, not necessarily denoting a common ethnicity. In modern times, some tribal names are still in use, but not in quite the same way, demonstrating behaviour rather than ethnic origins. Goths no longer pour across the Danube into the Roman Empire, but their modern namesakes dress in black clothes with shiny buckles and wear lots of black eye make-up, and Vandals do not invade Roman Africa from Spain, but they allegedly wreck bus shelters and produce graffiti on walls and trains (some of it quite artistic). Scythians are hardly ever heard of nowadays, but perhaps unfortunately the all-embracing label that the Greeks applied to a group of Iron Age tribes has now become embedded in modern culture. Perhaps the best way to excuse the continuing use of the term 'Celtic' is to make a comparison with the descriptive term European, which denotes a collection of people now settled within several different territories with firmly defined but not immutable boundaries, speaking different languages and following different customs, but all held together under a descriptive term within a larger geographical area. The origins, racial characteristics, customs and languages of Europeans differ, but the people also share enough common denominators besides their geographical location to justify the label.

There is a strong tradition that Celtic Iron Age peoples of Europe often worshipped and carried out their religious ceremonies in the open air. This probably arises from the works of Greek and Roman authors who observed and described their practices, referring to sacred groves and describing the rituals, often grisly, that were observed there. The Greeks and Romans lived in towns and built temples to their gods. The Celtic Iron Age tribes had only just begun to develop in this direction when the classical writers encountered them.

It may well be the case that at Bath, where the hot springs bubbled forth, the natives came and went, perhaps bathed in the waters to cure various ailments, and also celebrated their annual festivals and important rituals, without the benefit of any structures to honour the deity or to provide a focus for offerings and sacrifices. It is certainly true that up to the present time, no traces of any pre-Roman Iron Age buildings have been found in the vicinity of the springs in Bath. This does not mean that there were never any buildings before the Romans arrived, but since archaeologists have not been able to excavate the whole of the city of Bath, it can only be said that no Iron Age building has been found up to now.

The only indication that the Iron Age people used the area is the gravel causeway found during excavation of part of the site.[3]

It was found when the King's Bath was excavated and the mud of the spring was dug out. The pathway had been built with layers of rubble and gravel, all held in place by small stakes along the edges, which stopped the water from washing it all away. Eighteen Celtic coins were found in the vicinity, indicating that offerings were made to the deity of the springs, perhaps to give thanks or to make a request for help. The establishment of a causeway implies communal effort and organisation, and a sufficiently high number of visitors to warrant the building and maintenance of the path.

The users may have belonged to a single tribe, who claimed the land as their own. Alternatively the springs may have been an important cult centre and the visitors may have been drawn from much wider areas beyond Bath. It is not known if there was also a person or a group of people in charge of access to and from the springs and their use. If so, it would imply residence nearby and probably even an Iron Age version of regular opening hours.

It is worth repeating that the lack of any archaeological evidence for a pre-Roman shrine at Bath does not mean that nothing was ever built. Excavation is notoriously difficult in towns which have been built up for hundreds of years. Most excavations in these circumstances have to wait for a suitable opportunity to dig when some structure is being pulled down and another one is to be built. It is therefore a random and completely arbitrary affair to choose the places to excavate, and there is also considerable pressure to complete the work in the usually small window of opportunity, in the interval after the demolition squads have done their work, and before the developers start theirs. For developers it is also an anxious time, because one of the ways in which a dig might be prolonged is the discovery of a cemetery, in which case the bodies are to be treated with respect, excavated slowly and carefully, studied in detail, and eventually reburied, or placed in museums. Even so, time is usually short for archaeologists, and digs are usually confined to relatively small areas. The places where archaeologists would like to dig are only very rarely offered, in extremely unusual circumstances. When York Minster required underpinning and repair some years ago, a part of the headquarters of the Roman legionary fortress came to light, and though it would probably have been much less expensive to fill in the whole area after the structural work was completed, the remains of Roman and later buildings have been conserved and explained for visitors. In Bath, few such opportunities are available. The larger and more important historic buildings have tended to cluster around the springs, exactly where the larger and more important Roman buildings were sited. For instance it would be nice to know what is underneath the abbey at Bath, not just in a trench or two, but under the whole of it and the precincts surrounding it. There may be a continuing, possibly unbroken, tradition of worship of some deity or deities on this site from prehistoric times to the present day. However, applications to pull down the abbey need not be considered.

The Roman structures at Bath have been investigated as far as possible, but underneath them, still undetected because it is not possible to disturb the buildings to investigate the ancient ground levels, there may be evidence of a pre-Roman shrine to Sulis. It would probably not need to be sited precisely at the springs, which might explain why no buildings came to light when the causeway giving access to the water was investigated. At other Romano-British temples and shrines, where a native British god or goddess is equated with a Roman one, it is becoming clear that worship in the open air was not necessarily the norm, and under the foundations of the Roman buildings there were indeed native British shrines. Some of these sites may have been considered sacred places for thousands of years.

One of the most famous sites where an Iron Age shrine was converted into a Romano-British temple is Hayling Island, where the native British circular shrine within a rectangular enclosure was rebuilt on a larger scale but in exactly the same fashion by the Romans of the late first century AD.[4] At Uley in Gloucestershire, there is evidence of Neolithic activity in the vicinity of a later hill-fort, and not far from the hill-fort an Iron Age shrine in a rectangular enclosure was discovered, lying underneath the Roman temple, which was built on much the same pattern as its native British predecessor.[5] Several Iron Age coins were found, indicating that the pre-Roman British tribesmen and women made offerings there. At Harlow in Essex, where Bronze Age burials have been found, and several Iron Age coins, the Romano-British temple of the later first century AD succeeded an Iron Age shrine dedicated to an unknown deity, but more recently the discovery of a stone head of the Roman goddess Minerva suggests that, as at Bath, the Celtic deity was a local goddess whose attributes could be comfortably equated with those of Minerva.[6] There may be more Iron Age shrines awaiting discovery underneath later Roman versions in the countryside and in Romano-British towns. In some cases Iron Age shrines may have been tentatively identified as dwelling places, because on plan the houses and shrines look quite similar. Not all sites have been fully excavated, either because they are inaccessible, or because in order to find out what existed underneath a Roman temple it is necessary to destroy it to get down to previous levels. Continuity of worship at some of these Iron Age and Roman sites is suggested by the presence of finds from the Neolithic period and the Bronze Age. It cannot be proven conclusively that the earlier prehistoric people actually worshipped or performed ceremonies at the sites, but it is a profound thought that some places in Britain may have been held sacred for millennia rather than centuries. In the fifth century AD a Christian basilica church was built over the Roman temple at Uley. A statue of Mercury belonging to the former temple was buried, perhaps with some respect, before the Christian building was erected. It is fascinating to think that people may have honoured their ancestors and their gods on this site since 4000 BC or even earlier. It may be that they had also worshipped in the same way and for a similarly long period at Bath, where the hot springs gushed out of the ground with such abundance. To the prehistoric people who visited the springs, it would have been a mystical place imbued with religious connotations, surely the preserve of some important deity who presided over the waters. When the Romans arrived on the scene, it may be that the temples and baths that they built continued a tradition that was already thousands of years old.

2

THE ROMANS ARRIVE

Long before the Emperor Claudius set in motion the invasion and conquest of Britain in AD 43, the tribes who inhabited the island were well aware of Rome, and the Romans were equally well acquainted with the tribes. This may hold true only for the British tribes of the south, while further north the native people may not have had direct dealing with Rome except remotely, through trade or hearsay.

From at least the fourth century BC if not earlier, the Greeks of the colony of Marseilles knew about Britain. Sailors and traders visited the island; some of them may have penetrated inland beyond the coasts and harbours and some of them may have explored the seas all around the island. There may have been several written accounts of such voyages, but the only one of which there is any knowledge is that of Pytheas, most of whose work is lost, but sections of it survive in extracts quoted or reported by other authors. Later Greek and Roman authors made use of Pytheas's account mostly to disagree with what he said.

Other ancient authors who wrote about Britain include Diodorus Siculus and Strabo, who wrote in Greek in the first century BC, and Pliny, whose Latin works belong to the first century AD. These writers had not necessarily seen the island for themselves. The first writer of note who did see a small part of the island was Gaius Julius Caesar. He was proconsul of Gaul, and was engaged in subduing the Gallic tribes when he launched two short-lived invasions of Britain in 55 and 54 BC. His excuse for leaving his province of Gaul, which he was not supposed to do without permission from the Roman Senate, was that the British tribes were sending aid to the Gauls.

Caesar's Expeditions to Britain

The two invasions of 55 and 54 BC, described in Caesar's *Gallic War*, were probably not intended to form the basis of permanent conquest and occupation. They served a different purpose in bringing the exploits of Gaius Julius Caesar to the attention of the Roman public. Fortuitously his commentaries on his campaigns also furnish modern historians with a valuable description of Britain and some of its inhabitants in the first century BC. The reliability of Caesar's work has been questioned, but apart from archaeological evidence it is all that there is for the period. Later authors of the first three centuries AD did not substantially alter or augment what Caesar tells us.

During his two expeditions, Caesar gained first-hand experience of the tribes of the south and south-east of Britain. His description of the tribes beyond the areas that he had seen for himself is based on hearsay. Some of the tribes for which he provides names are not securely located, nor do these tribal names appear in any other ancient historical work. This does not necessarily mean that Caesar was completely mistaken or that he deliberately falsified anything in his account. As noted in the previous chapter, tribal society was not fixed or immutable. It is possible that when the

Romans annexed the island of Britain, nearly a century after Caesar's expeditions, these tribes that he had heard about had been subsumed or even annihilated by more powerful neighbours.

Caesar's brief description cannot be used to elucidate what was happening in the south-west areas of Britain, and in particular the area around Bath. It is not even known for certain which tribe or tribes were settled in the region of Bath in the first century BC. Conversely, tribal knowledge of Rome was probably already firmly entrenched. Apart from the benefit of traveller's tales and exchange of news, these tribes, or at least their elite leaders, could have been receiving Roman goods through Gaul, since traders had been crossing the Channel for some considerable time. A sophisticated trading depot had been flourishing at Hengistbury Head for several years, and was later to be replaced by another at Poole. In more than one passage in *Gallic War*, Caesar himself explicitly states that the Veneti, a tribe of excellent seafarers and navigators living on the coast of Gaul, regularly sailed to and from Britain to exploit the trading possibilities there. They were opposed to Caesar's ventures in case their trade should be disrupted.

After Caesar's conquest of Gaul the whole country was divided up into Roman provinces. With a Roman presence just across the Channel, trade continued to and from Britain, and probably increased, with the inclusion of a larger number of Roman goods shipped from Gallic ports. Judging from abundant archaeological remains of amphorae and other vessels, the tribes of the south and south-east of Britain developed an insatiable taste for Roman wine, and they readily acquired luxury items such as glassware and jewellery. During the first century BC some of the tribes had developed their own coinage, based on Greek models. Shortly before the Roman conquest, some tribes with closer contacts with Rome began to use Latin words on their coins. In the reign of Augustus, Epillus, the chief of the Atrebates, described himself 'REX CALLE', king of Calleva, and his successor, called Verica, minted coins with a horseman on the obverse, with the title 'REX' underneath the horse's hooves. The use of the title may indicate that the chiefs had received recognition of their status from the Roman government. These enterprising tribes may have traded with more distant ones in Britain, redistributing the goods they received from Roman sources. It is possible that the people of Bath had indirect contact with Rome through trade with their neighbours, or even direct contact via ports on the south coast, but without firm evidence this must remain merely a possibility.

Britain and Rome in the Last Century of the Iron Age

In the hundred years or so between the expeditions of Caesar of the mid-first century BC and the Roman conquest and occupation of Britain in the mid-first century AD, contact between the British tribes and Rome was maintained. This was on an individual tribal basis, since there was no sense of unity or of British nationalism among the Iron Age people. There may have been some uniformity of language, customs and overall religious beliefs, but people belonged first and foremost to a tribe with its leader, its territory, and its own gods and goddesses, all of which were of far greater importance to them than any ideology relating to the country of 'Britannia' as the Romans called it.

According to Strabo, who wrote his *Geography* in the later first century BC, British chiefs regularly sent diplomatic embassies to

Rome and made votive offerings in the temples of the Capitol, so much so that it was as if the whole island was already part of Roman property.[1] But Strabo's judgement was that there was nothing to be gained by annexing and administering Britain. He pointed out that the Britons succumbed quite readily to Roman taxation. They paid tax on goods inwards, consisting of wine and luxury goods, and also on goods being exported, which included slaves, hides, hunting dogs, grain and precious metals. The Romans could obtain what they wanted from Britain without the bother of invading, conquering, pacifying and administering the island. Strabo insisted that the cost of maintaining an army in Britain to oversee the collection of taxes would diminish or eradicate the value of these taxes that were already accruing to Rome with very little difficulty. Another reason why conquest was not necessary was that the British tribes scarcely posed any threat to Rome itself, or even to the province of Gaul across the Channel.

From around 50 BC to 30 BC, during the prolonged civil wars between Caesar and Pompey, and then between Caesar's successors, his great-nephew Octavian and Mark Antony, Britain was hardly a priority for the Romans. When Octavian had defeated Antony and Cleopatra, and established peace in Rome if not in all the provinces, he became the de facto ruler of the Roman Empire, though he would not have called himself Emperor in the sense that we use the term nowadays. His rule was bestowed on him by the compliant Senate, usually for a specified five- or ten-year term, so that by setting a temporal limit to his powers it did not seem that Octavian wished to establish a permanent dictatorship. The dictatorship for life had been awarded to Caesar, and the result was that shortly afterwards he had been assassinated by a few staunch Republicans who imagined that everyone else thought as they did. Therefore they made no plans to take over the state, because after all that would have been to act as dictators themselves. But the Republic did not spring back to life as it was before. The consul Mark Antony took charge, with considerable credit for avoiding an immediate bloodbath. He abolished the actual office of Dictator, but Octavian knew that there are more ways of becoming a dictator than by adopting the title. He played it slowly and safely, and the Senate renewed his powers when necessary. In 27 BC the Senate awarded him the title Augustus, which became part of the Imperial name.

Concerning Britain during the lifetime of Augustus, it was taken as read that at some time in the future, the island would be conquered and added to the Empire. Augustan literature reflected this surmise, but if such was the intention, several opportunities to conquer Britain were lost or ignored. According to the third-century historian Dio, there were three occasions when Octavian-Augustus could have launched an invasion of Britain. In 34, 27 and 26 BC, Augustus may have been preparing to invade Britain, but on each of these occasions a rebellion or some trouble in other provinces prevented him from doing so.[2] This allegedly frustrated thirst for conquest may be just wishful thinking on the part of Dio, who lived at a time when expansion of the Empire was regarded as the ultimate aim, especially during the reign of Severus.

On two occasions, not precisely dated, Augustus himself records in his memorial of his reign, known as *Res Gestae*, that among the several foreign rulers who appealed to him for assistance, there were two British chieftains who had been expelled from their kingdoms.[3] No precise dates are available, but the two events probably occurred in the late first century BC, or at least some time before Augustus wrote his memoir around AD 7. One of the British kings was Dubnovellaunus of the Trinovantes, whose centre was at Colchester. The more aggressive Catuvellauni took over the place, establishing their own capital there. For the other British chieftain, only part of his name survives, because neither the Latin nor the Greek text of *Res Gestae* preserves more than the first letters, 'Tin'. This used to be restored as Tincommius, an interpretation based on the name of one of Caesar's associates called Commius, king of the Atrebates in Gaul, who eventually ruled the Atrebates in Britain. More recently, coin finds from the territory of the British Atrebates, with the ruler's name in full, have established that Tincomarus is the true interpretation. But despite these inviting opportunities to interfere in British affairs, no invasion of Britain followed.

Similarly, there was no military expedition to assist the exiled Adminius, son of Cunobelinus, chief of the Catuvellauni. Adminius was forced out of Britain and came with his entourage to the Emperor Caligula in AD 39 while he was leading an expedition to Germany. Allegedly Caligula accepted the surrender of Adminius and his British retinue as though he had won over the whole island, and he even sent a letter to the consuls in Rome announcing it as such. This may or may not have been the context for the scarcely explicable gathering of Roman troops on the shores of Germany, as reported by Suetonius.[4] The Emperor drew up his artillery as if poised for attack, and then ordered the return to Rome with trophies of sea-shells from the beaches, the spoils of the ocean, as he called it. The whole episode probably had nothing to do with Britain, perhaps another garbled story about the mad Caligula, concerning whom nothing was too outrageous to believe. Again, as under Augustus, despite the reasonable political excuse offered by the exiled Adminius, no invasion of Britain followed.

Prelude to the Claudian Invasion

British tribal society during the Iron Age was dynamic but restless. A chieftain was only as strong as his own right arm and his ability to command loyal service from his warriors. A son succeeding his father was not automatically accepted as ruler until he proved himself strong enough to rule and protect his people, and there were plenty of rivals with the ambition and the power to oust him.

The Romans subscribed to the concept of the noble savage, and the historian Tacitus used it to good effect to contrast the nobility of the tribesmen with the decadence of Rome, but it is probably true to say that Britons were both noble and savage. Internal unrest within a tribe was common if not constant, and some rulers were expelled by their own tribesmen. Cunobelinus forced his son Adminius out of his territory before the Roman conquest, and such upheavals were still going on when the Romans had started to consolidate their hold on the southern half of the island after AD 43. In the Pennine areas the large federation of the Brigantes controlled a large territory ruled by their queen, Cartimandua, who had probably allied herself to Rome at the start of the conquest. She was allowed to rule her kingdom without too much Roman interference for nearly a decade, until in the early AD 50s her husband Venutius raised rebellion and forced her to seek refuge with the Romans. The governor Didius Gallus had to mount an expedition to rescue her.

Expansion of territory and the establishment of control over other tribes constituted just as much of an imperative for some of the British chiefs as it did for the Romans. Some tribal rulers were toppled when a stronger rival took over their land and people. Tribal names were not permanent, but could change as part of political upheavals or the amalgamation of separate groups. As mentioned above in Caesar's account of his British expeditions, he names some smaller tribes who are never heard of again and do not seem to have been present when the Romans conquered the island, so it is likely that these people were overtaken and absorbed, or possibly annihilated, by other tribes. In Germany in the third century AD, a new tribe called the Alamanni appeared, but their name carried no indication of racial origin. It was merely a result of a political confederation of different tribes under a name that simply meant 'All Men'. In Britain in the third century AD, Cassius Dio refers to the tribes of the Maeatae and Caledonii, with the added information that they had absorbed lesser tribes, though it can only be guessed what the previous names of the smaller tribes or the confederations had been.

One example of British territorial aggression and expansion is well known. The Trinovantian capital at Colchester was taken over by Cunobelinus, the chief of the Catuvellauni. This tribe was originally based at Verlamion, which became the Roman Verulamium. In the course of their expansion, the Catuvellauni had gained control of most of the lands north of the Thames by the mid-AD 30s, and they made the erstwhile Trinovantian capital of Colchester one of their own main centres and minted coins there. A takeover such as this was probably not normally a peaceful affair of negotiation and mutual agreement. Some chieftains and their people were probably wiped out, but the

British tribal refugees who survived, such as Dubnovellaunus, Tincomarus and Adminius, show that British chiefs who were expelled and escaped intact knew what to do when this occurred. They went to Rome.

The Emperor Claudius and the Invasion of Britain

Not long after the assassination of Caligula and the accession of Claudius, a displaced British ruler of the Atrebates called Verica, or Berikos or Bericus according to Dio,[5] arrived at Rome to appeal for help. This time, in AD 43, the Emperor responded, and sent four legions and accompanying auxiliary troops under his general Aulus Plautius to invade Britain. The reasons why Claudius took the bait and decided to conquer Britain have been attributed to his desire to achieve military glory to elevate himself to the level of Tiberius and Augustus. Although a member of the Imperial family, he was a most unlikely Emperor, long overlooked, except for a few relatively unimportant official appointments in Rome. He was scholarly and clever, but he was physically unprepossessing because of his lame leg and his stammer, and allegedly he drooled a little as well. This did not seem to bother the soldiers of the Imperial bodyguard who found him hiding behind a curtain, fearing for his life, after the assassination of his nephew, the Emperor Caligula. The German soldiers regarded him as a member of the Imperial family and hailed him as Emperor, and the Senate and people accepted him as such.

Claudius became Emperor by accident, but he made a creditable job of it. He had no experience of commanding armies, but his desire for military glory is revealed by his assiduous collecting of Imperial salutations as Imperator. This title was awarded by spontaneous acclamation of the soldiers to a commander after a military victory; it derives from the term *Imperium*, denoting powers bestowed by the Senate on generals who had been given the command of armies during the Republic. In the Empire, acclamations were reserved for the Imperial family, and any subordinate general who allowed the troops to salute him in this manner risked the charge of treason. The title Imperator became part of the Imperial nomenclature, along with Augustus and Caesar, whose names became titles. The title Caesar survived until the twentieth century as the German Kaiser and the Russian Tsar. The Emperor Claudius received more Imperial salutations than most other Emperors, twenty-seven in total, not bad for a neglected relative of Augustus, Tiberius and Caligula, a man who read books and studied history, who had never seen any military action.

The simple explanation that Claudius had an overwhelming desire for military achievement cannot have been the only reason why he decided to add Britain to the Empire. The project had, after all, been on the cards since the early days of Augustus, at least in literary circles and popular imagination. Traders and merchants were no doubt keen to gain a more secure foothold in the island, too. They were already there by proxy if not in actuality. The harbour at Fishbourne has yielded many Roman finds of the pre-invasion period, and it is suggested that a Roman base may have been established there before the conquest. There may also have been a Roman trading establishment at Colchester before the Claudian fort was built there. Future excavations at other sites may further elucidate these suggestions. But it is clear that Britain and Rome were already linked, and if Claudius had not undertaken the annexation, it may only have been a matter of time before another Emperor did so. In Claudius's day, the timing was good if not ideal, because the Rhineland was more or less pacified, the troops stationed there were available, and it was always a good idea to keep the soldiers fully occupied.

AD 43 and Afterwards

The story of the Roman invasion of Britain in AD 43 has been told many times over, so this account will enumerate only the salient points, and their implications for the area around Bath. The troops who had been assembled for the invasion clearly did not want to go to Britain, but Claudius's freedman secretary Narcissus talked them round. Their reluctance illustrates the fact that despite the existing Roman contact with the island, it was uncharted territory as far as the soldiers were concerned, but their greater concerns more likely revolved around leaving their bases on the Rhine and probably their unofficial and unauthorised families.

Much ink has been spilled and several keyboards pounded in an attempt to locate the landing site, or sites, on the south coast. Richborough features largely in this speculation, but as yet the necessary archaeological evidence is lacking. The Britons did not oppose the landings in strength. After looking for and eventually finding an enemy to fight, Plautius moved towards the territory of the Catuvellauni across the River Thames, and halted there, officially to consolidate his gains and to work out how to conquer the next territories, but in reality to await the visitation of Claudius, who arrived in style with his retinue, and some war elephants to impress the Britons. He received the submission of the Catuvellauni and planted a fort in their capital at Camulodunum (modern Colchester). According to the fragmentary inscription in the Capitoline Museum in Rome, he received the submission of eleven tribes in total, though this may not have happened all at once. Unfortunately the tribes who submitted are not named in the inscription, so as one historian has famously said, it has never been harder to find a British first eleven. One of this first eleven may have been Togidubnus, who may have lived in the first villa at Fishbourne and who may also have been instrumental in founding the town and spa at Bath. Claudius remained in the south-east for sixteen days, and returned to Rome, leaving Plautius to get on with the conquest.

The number of troops in Plautius's initial force is not precisely known. There will have been a number of auxiliary units, composed of non-Romans and often raised by levying tribesmen from inside and outside the Empire. These units may not have reached the standard organisation that they later possessed, but in general they were either 500 or 1,000 strong, some of them cavalry and some of them infantry, and sometimes part mounted units which contained infantry and horsemen. Virtually nothing is known of which units accompanied the invasion armies. It is traditionally stated that four legions were sent to Britain, II Augusta, IX Hispana, XIV Gemina, and XX, which had no victory titles until after the Boudiccan rebellion in AD 60–61, when it became XX Valeria Victrix. At the same time, XIV Gemina was awarded the titles Martia Victrix. These legions are attested in Britain by inscriptions set up at a later time, so it is assumed that they were the ones taking part in the invasion. Not all of them are represented among the inscriptions found at Bath.

The only one of these four legions for which there is corroborative evidence is II Augusta, whose claim to fame at this early period is owed to the fact that it was commanded by the legionary legate Titus Flavius Vespasianus, who became Emperor of Rome in AD 69. This legion was probably the most prominent in the area around Bath in the early years of Roman rule, though it was probably not operating in isolation from the other legions. It is likely that Legio XX, or part of it, was based at the first legionary fortress at Kingsholm near Gloucester.

As soon as Aulus Plautius was in a position to do so, he ordered his legionary legates to fan out from the south-east, roughly towards Lincoln in the north, towards Wroxeter and the Midlands, and in the case of II Augusta to the south-west. Since Vespasian, the commander of II Augusta, later became Emperor, his early exploits were recorded by later Greek and Roman historians, whereas very little is known of the other legionary legates. Most famously Vespasian's activities probably included the attack on the hill-fort of Maiden Castle in Dorset.

In the initial stages of the conquest of Britain the legions and the unknown numbers of accompanying auxiliary troops probably did not march as single units, but would be split up into smaller detachments, called vexillations, to take and hold various points for a short time. The early situation of the Roman armies in Britain would have been far from static, with different detachments from the legions and from the auxiliary troops operating simultaneously in several different locations. They would build forts of timber with earth ramparts, which would be occupied for a short time for a specific purpose, and then the troops would move on. Each legion and auxiliary unit would require a headquarters base where records were kept and the administrative work was done, but even these bases need not have been long-term affairs in the early years after the invasion.

Excavations of early Roman forts have revealed tantalising evidence that legionaries and auxiliary troops were sometimes brigaded together, though this evidence is limited to pieces of legionary and auxiliary equipment, as at the small fort at Hod Hill. This is a possible indication of mixed troops, but not of their proportions, their status, or the duration of their stay. In more fortunate cases an inscription turns up mentioning different kinds of troops. It has to be admitted that a piece of equipment normally identifiable as an attribute of an auxiliary soldier, or an inscription actually naming a cavalry trooper or infantry soldier in an otherwise legionary context, does not mean that the whole unit or even a part of it was stationed with the whole or a part of a legion.

The Romans in the Area Around Bath in the Early First Century AD

All around the wider area encircling Bath, the Romans were actively engaged in building forts from the first years after the invasion. It is probable that they took over the whole region as early as the winter of AD 43. At Alchester near Oxford, where excavations carried out in 2000 revealed a timber fort, dendro-chronological dating of the wood that was used to build the west gate has revealed that the trees were felled in AD 44. A tombstone of a veteran of Legio II Augusta was discovered at this site, which may imply that there was a detachment of this legion stationed there, but on the strength of one inscription no-one can be pedantic about the exact unit or units or the numbers of men involved, except to say that there was a military presence there of some kind.

Other early forts include Hod Hill in Dorset and Ham Hill in Somerset, where it was probably Vespasian's troops who utilised existing Iron Age hill-forts. The ditches that had already been dug by the early Britons served as ramparts on at least two sides of the Roman forts, thus sparing the soldiers from having to undertake a great deal of labour. About a mile north of Gloucester at Kingsholm, a fortress was established, around AD 49 if not earlier. It was sited close to an Iron Age settlement, and probably held soldiers from Legio XX, but perhaps not the entire legion. There may also have been the whole or part of an auxiliary unit.

Closer to Bath, and not far from a British settlement at Bagendon, which the Romans called an *oppidum*, a Roman fort was built at what would later become the town of Cirencester, though the exact foundation date of the first fort is not known. It was soon replaced by a second fort to house a cavalry unit, sited a little further to the north-west of the original site. At the mouth of the River Avon, north-west of Bath, the port at Sea Mills was established, taking its Roman name Abona, or Portus Abonae, from the British word Avon, which in a variety of Celtic languages simply means 'river'. In Welsh it is Afon, in Cornish Avon, in Breton Aven, and in Irish it is Abann, which explains why there are several rivers called Avon in Britain.

A short distance to the north-west of Bath, in the Mendips, the Romans quickly established lead mines around Charterhouse. Lead had many uses in the Roman Empire, for the manufacture of pewter and the extraction of silver, and also for more mundane uses for all aspects of plumbing, which is derived from the Latin for lead, *plumbum*. When the bathing establishments of Aquae Sulis were first built, the lead from these mines would be used to line the tanks and make the water pipes. The Romans were extracting the lead from Charterhouse at least by AD 49 if not earlier. Dating evidence is derived from a lead ingot, found in the sixteenth century, 5 miles south of Charterhouse near Wookey Hole.[6] Unfortunately it is now lost, but it was described by the antiquarian John Leland, who toured Britain in the Tudor period. He transcribed the inscription, on what he described as an oblong tablet of lead (*oblonga plumbi tabula*), as 'TI. CLAUD. CAESAR. AUG. P. M. TR.P. VIIII. IMP. XVI. DE BRITAN'. The customarily abbreviated Latin translates into English as 'Tiberius Claudius Caesar Augustus, Pontifex Maximus, with tribunician power for the ninth year, Imperator for the sixteenth time, from [lead mines] in Britain'. Leland was generally conscientious and trustworthy, and the details can be taken as correct. The inscription is very important because it records features which provide the date AD 49, namely the ninth year of Claudius's tribunician power (*tribunicia potestas*, abbreviated on inscriptions as 'TRIB. POT.' or in this case as 'TR.P.'). This gave the Emperors many of their legal powers without the necessity of actually holding the office of tribune, and was renewed annually from 10 December, therefore it is highly useful in dating inscriptions, in a similar fashion to the dating of documents by the regnal years of medieval kings and queens.

Another lead ingot from Blagdon in Somerset, near the Charterhouse mines, is more problematical.[7] It was discovered by a ploughman in 1853, and unfortunately part of its inscription was damaged by the plough. The date is the same as the Wookey Hole ingot, if the lettering on the side of the ingot is correctly interpreted. The letters 'V.ETP' and 'V.ETP.C' possibly refer to the consuls Veranius and Pompeius, who held office in Rome in AD 49.

For the major inscription on this same lead ingot, various interpretations have been suggested, some of them attempting to link the ingot with the presence of II Augusta in the mining region. The words 'BRITANNIC AUG' are clear enough but the two letters that follow are damaged, giving enough leeway for interpreters to state that the latter part of the inscription is meant to read 'AUG. LEG. II', indicating that soldiers of Legio II Augusta were supervising the works. On the one hand this is not the usual formula, which is more commonly written 'LEG. II AUG', but on the other hand it would be usual for the army to be involved with the convoying of the lead if not the supervision of the mining of it, and if the military were involved then it would most likely be II Augusta. The jury is still out on whether some of the soldiers of this legion really were operating at the lead mines not far away from Bath.

An Early Roman Fort at Bath?

With all the Roman activity around Bath, it is to be expected that there would be a military presence somewhere around the hot springs, most likely hidden underneath the extended modern town rather than some distance away from it. The site of Bath in the loop of the River Avon would have been an important one for the Romans in the early years after the conquest. Three major Roman roads converged here, at a convenient crossing point of the river. One route connects London with the port at Sea Mills at the mouth of the Avon. This road runs through Silchester and Mildenhall. Another route runs south-eastwards to the harbour at Poole in Dorset. The third route is the Fosse Way, running diagonally across the country from the south-west towards the north-east, connecting the legionary fortresses of Exeter and Lincoln. These early fortresses were built around AD 55 or possibly a little earlier, so the Fosse Way was presumably established at the same time.

There has been great debate about this road, mostly concerning its purpose. It was once suggested that it was intended to act as a permanent frontier, implying that the Romans had taken in as much of Britain as they wanted and had decided to fortify the route dividing the more Romanised and profitable south-east from the non-Romanised Midlands and the north. This opinion was later revised by an alternative suggestion that the Fosse Way simply marked the point where the Romans had got up to for the time being, south of which they were prepared to consolidate, control and administer, and north of which they could influence and possibly exploit, until such time as they were ready to take on the rest of the island. In this case the road would be guarded and patrolled like any other border, but the intention behind it was not to call a halt to the conquest. Currently the Fosse Way is not regarded as a frontier at all, definitely not such a firmly demarcated line such as Hadrian established in Britain in the second century AD. In any case, at this early stage in the conquest it would have been quite anachronistic to create a frontier beyond which there was no intention to advance. The Romans thought of their Empire as territory without end (*Imperium sine fine* in Latin), and this meant no end in the territorial sense, or in fact the temporal sense.

Another factor that weighs against the concept of a frontier is that beyond the Fosse Way there were deposits of gold in South Wales at Dolaucothi, and lead in Flintshire and Derbyshire, all of which were exploited as soon as the Romans were able to do so. It is likely that the Roman governors were informed about the locations of the mineral wealth of the island from an early date, and the best way to extract it was to annexe the territory rather than trying to carry out mining operations without fully controlling the areas around the mines. The Fosse Way was probably neither a permanent frontier nor a temporary stopping place, but merely a communications and transport route linking the two major fortresses at Exeter and Lincoln, giving access to all areas on both sides of the road.

Whatever the designated purpose of the Fosse Way, the spacing of the Roman military installations along this route would suggest that there was a fort at Bath. The crossing of the Avon and the convergence of three routes would also suggest that the Romans would have guarded the place. Modern archaeologists and historians are convinced that there must have been a fort somewhere in or near Bath. But so far not one single piece of evidence has been found that there was one, and although archaeology itself is not an exact science, 'must have been' is even less exact. One day some proof of an early Roman military presence may be discovered in Bath.

It would help considerably if the exact course of the three major routes to and through Bath were known, but these too are uncertain, and it is not known precisely where or how the roads crossed the river. It is suggested that the ford at Cleveland Bridge would have been the principal place where the Avon was crossed, and there may have been another crossing point to the south-west.[8] If a fort could be identified, it would help to indicate, if not prove, where the roads entered and left the area, or conversely if one or more of the routes could be definitely established it might help to locate the postulated fort. It has been suggested that the roads converged at Bathwick, and there would have been a fort there.[9] One piece of evidence that may be relevant is a tombstone from Bath of a soldier of Legio XX[10] which is listed without its battle honours, Valeria Victrix, which the legion was awarded after the rebellion of Boudicca in AD 60–61. The stone was found in the sixteenth century and is now lost, but the drawing of it has been reproduced from the work of the antiquarian John Horsley. If the victory titles Valeria Victrix, usually abbreviated to VV, had been present on the stone, it is unlikely that they would have been missed off the drawing, but even so the absence of the honorary titles do not necessarily prove that the tomb was set up before AD 60, because other inscriptions of Legio XX have been found, clearly dated to a period *after* AD 60, which still lack the Valeria Victrix suffix. It remains a tantalising but unproven implication that some soldiers of Legio XX were stationed at Bath before AD 60. This would be about fifteen years before the temple and bath complex was built in the last quarter of the first century AD.

The fort at Bath or possibly Bathwick would have been built of timber with ramparts of earth, surrounded by one or more ditches, with breaks for the gateways, usually four, one on each side of the fort. Roman forts were not generally stone-built until the early second century, under the Emperor Trajan. It is not to be expected that there would be any trace of stone walls or internal buildings on the site of the supposed fort at Bath. If there was a fort, it was presumably demolished, or at least demilitarised, when the temple and bath complex was built, so trying to detect it, even if land should suddenly become available for excavation at Bathwick or anywhere else in Bath, would be difficult.

There are certain tell-tale signs to look for. When the Romans abandoned a fort, they sometimes razed it and burnt the timbers that could not be used again, and put their rubbish, broken pottery and the like, into the curved ends of the ditches on either side of the gateways, and then filled them in. If the fort was to be given over to civilian development, as for instance at Gloucester, where the first inhabitants were legionary veterans, the defences, internal roads and barracks might be left standing and then gradually altered as time went on, and the settlement gradually became less like a fort and more like a civilian town. Since no-one knows what happened at Bath, or where exactly the fort would have been sited, or whether it was destroyed or used at first for settlers, the signs of early military occupation will be hard to find, consisting probably of post-holes for the barracks and administrative buildings; some evidence of ditches, with rubbish deposits if the excavators should be lucky enough to find the curved ends of a ditch; possibly some signs of a bonfire in the middle of the fort; and maybe a scatter of small finds such as coins and pieces of equipment. The discovery of any one of these would be extremely gratifying.

The Later First-Century Military Situation Around Bath

After the invasion under Claudius, the Romans moved gradually northwards and westwards to take over Wales and much of the Midlands. The north was ruled at first by the queen of the Brigantes, Cartimandua, allied to Rome, so the Romans kept out of her territory except to watch it from its southern borders. There was probably a military presence in the south-west and around Bath for much of this time.

The conquest of Wales during the AD 50s was arduous. Two governors died in office, and the resistance of the Silures in South Wales and the Ordovices further north was vigorous and prolonged. In the reign of Nero, just as the governor Suetonius Paullinus was ready to take over North Wales, where he waged war against the British tribes in Snowdonia and specifically the Druids congregated on Anglesey, the south-eastern parts of Britain erupted in a fierce rebellion under Boudicca, the queen of the Iceni, in AD 60 and 61. The damage was extensive, the casualties high and reinforcements had to be sent from Germany to shore up the numbers of troops. For the next decade there seems to have been only consolidation in Britain, and no thought of military advance. Towards the end of the decade the Romans started to fight each other in a civil war that resulted from a desire on the part of four different military commanders to rid the Empire of Nero, with the assistance of their provincial armies. In AD 68 Nero committed suicide, and the short-lived Emperors Galba, Otho, and Vitellius took power one after the other, until Vespasian arrived and calmed everything down in AD 69. In the AD 70s, the conquest of Wales was resumed and the conquest of the north began.

Under the three Flavian Emperors, Titus Flavius Vespasianus (AD 69–79) and his two sons, Titus (AD 79–81) and Domitian (AD 81–96) there was a continuous military advance, taking in Wales and the north as far as Scotland, until disastrous events on the Danube forced Domitian and his successors Nerva and Trajan to call a halt and withdraw into the north of England so as to be able to remove some of the troops for the Danube campaigns. The tremendous advance in northern Britain was due to three dynamic governors appointed by Vespasian and Titus. The first was Petillius Cerialis, who concentrated on northern areas, probably campaigning beyond Carlisle, followed by Sextus Julius Frontinus, who finally defeated and pacified the Silures of South Wales, and then Gnaeus Julius Agricola, who completed the conquest of northern England and Scotland. This governor is better known than any other because his son-in-law was the historian Tacitus, who left an account of Agricola's military campaigns and his encouragement and development of civilian affairs in Britain.

While these campaigns were continuing, the legions and auxiliary troops moved out of the south-west and re-established themselves in new bases. Many of these are known, but although legionary bases and auxiliary forts can be identified, dating them precisely is not always possible, and discerning which units occupied them is even more difficult. All around Bath there would be movement and change. The brief overview given here is based on informed speculation derived from the recent work of archaeologists and historians, and will be susceptible to revision if more information comes to light.

The fortress at Exeter was probably founded around AD 55 and occupied by Legio II Augusta, until around AD 75, when the legion was moved into South Wales as the campaigns were conducted there. The final legionary base of II Augusta was built at Caerleon. Legio XX was probably at Kingsholm until the later AD 50s, and then at the legionary base at Usk for the Welsh campaigns. Discharged veterans from this legion took up residence at the fortress at Gloucester, which was made a colony, or *colonia*, as was the fortress of Lincoln when its legion moved to a new fortress at York. Despite the fact that the colony at Gloucester was named for the Emperor Nerva, who reigned from AD 96 to 98, it has been argued that the colony was actually founded much earlier than this.[11] The important point for the history of Bath is that the legions moved west and north as the campaigns of the three Flavian governors were fought. The original four legions were reduced to three, and based at the three fortresses of Caerleon, Chester and York by the end of the AD 70s. The auxiliary troops also moved away. The fort at Cirencester was given up in the AD 70s, and the troops who may have been quartered in civilian settlements such as Silchester were relocated. The area around Bath was being de-militarised and was ripe for civilian development.

Civilian Development in the Areas Around Bath to *c.* AD 70

It is difficult if not impossible to discern how Bath itself and its environs were affected by the British rebellion under Boudicca, and then the Roman civil war of AD 69. At the lead mines around Charterhouse, it seems that throughout all this upheaval it was business as usual. Imperial control of the production of the Mendips had been relinquished either in whole or in part to a civilian contractor whose name, Nipius Ascanius, is found stamped on an ingot dating to the second half of AD 60.[12] This individual also conducted lead mining operations in Flintshire, perhaps around the same time.[13] There may have been plans to develop the area around Bath in general, and the hot springs in particular, that were frustrated by the Boudiccan rebellion and the slow recovery thereafter. For whatever reason, the building of the temples and bathing establishments had to wait until the middle years of the AD 70s. It is quite possible that the healing waters were being used for a few years without the benefit of public buildings or any structures at all, but there is as yet no archaeological clue that this may have been the case, apart from the causeway that was made in the later Iron Age. This causeway may still have been in use throughout the early Roman occupation. The presence of a fort need not have precluded approaches to the springs. Since three roads converged at Bath it is inconceivable that the hot springs could be completely ignored between AD 43 and around AD 75.

While the army was present in the wider area around Bath, the sites where forts were established attracted civilian settlement nearby. This was a normal development wherever the army was based, even if the bases were occupied for only a short time. The legionary and auxiliary soldiers were among the very few people in the Roman world who received pay. Everyone else derived an income from businesses, or from agriculture, or land or property ownership. The soldiers, more or less tied to their bases when they were not on active service, or absent on special missions or periods of extended leave, therefore had money to spend on whatever was for sale in their immediate locality. The civilians were not slow to take advantage of this fact. Those who made their homes near the forts may have been a mixed group of native Britons and non-native traders, but no-one can be certain of their origins because they left few records, or at least if they did set up inscriptions in these early years, few have been discovered.

The settlements that sprang up around Roman forts were called *vici*, and although there are very few personal records of individuals, the settlements eventually developed a corporate identity, as attested by inscriptions set up by the *vicani*, referring to the dwellers of the *vicus*. A *vicus* could also denote a rural village, or a section of a town, but in a military context it refers to the collection of civilian dwellings around a fort. During the early years of the conquest, there may have been several *vici* attached to the forts and fortresses where the army remained for longer than a few months, such as the legionary base at Exeter founded about AD 55, and the Kingsholm site at Gloucester. For Bath itself, since no fort has been discovered, there is also a dearth of evidence for a *vicus* that may have been established somewhere in the vicinity, but it is highly likely that there was one, given that the site was at or near the crossing point of the River Avon and three separate routes converged on it, bringing people to and through Bath, hopefully with money to spend.

The tribes of the later Iron Age who were settled in the territories around Bath included the Dobunni, and the Atrebates, and sometime after the Roman conquest, the Belgae. This last group of people may have been a mixed selection of natives who were brought in as settlers and given a newly created name. In the early years of the Roman occupation, it is not certain which tribes occupied the area that was later to be assigned to the Belgae, who were based around Winchester. One theory is that there were a number of smaller tribes, whose names are unknown and who were either dispossessed or annihilated when the Romans reorganised the area as the territory of the Belgae, but this development probably belongs to the period after AD 70.

It is not certain whether any of these tribes claimed the hot springs of Bath as their own, and though the boundaries between tribes on the eve of the Roman conquest can be roughly defined it is not possible to draw them in detail on a modern map. The Dobunni lived in the Cotswolds and around the upper reaches of the Thames. Apart from initial resistance from an anti-Roman faction, the majority of tribesmen of the Dobunni seem to have been compliant, causing little trouble and probably co-operating with the Romans from the beginning. Some of the tribe probably lived at the *oppidum* at Bagendon, which seems to have been abandoned between AD 60 and AD 70. It is suggested that the tribesmen left their native town and settled around the Roman fort at Cirencester, attracted by the opportunities to make money by selling goods and services to the soldiers.

Further away from Bath there were three important settlements dating from the Iron Age, which already displayed Romanising tendencies even in pre-Roman times and continued in occupation throughout the Roman invasion and conquest. It can only be speculated how much direct influence these Romanised settlements may have had on the development of Bath.

The town at Silchester was a centre of the Atrebates. It had already acquired its British name Calleva at least as early as the age of Augustus, as shown by the coinage of the British rulers of the Atrebates, Epillus and Verica. The latter king was driven out by the Catuvellauni when this aggressive tribe expanded and took over the town and surrounding territory.

From about the mid-AD 70s Silchester eventually became the capital of the Atrebates, called by its Roman name Calleva Atrebatum, but the town was already developing along Roman lines well before this. Even before the Roman conquest it had been developing as a pro-Roman Atrebatic state under its previous kings, who issued coins with Latin legends on them, and traded for Roman goods. A timber forum was built as early as AD 45, or at any rate early enough to warrant another timber rebuild before AD 96. The forum site was once thought to represent a military headquarters, but this theory has now been revised in favour of very early civilian development along Roman lines. The town also possessed an amphitheatre in the mid-50s and a bathing establishment as early as the reign of Nero, dating from about AD 65, but there was no Roman-style street-grid until after AD 70, with the result that the forum is not quite aligned to the later street layout.

An outstanding feature at Silchester is the series of earthwork defences, one of which is known in modern terminology as the Inner Earthwork, erected perhaps as early as AD 43. It appears that the ramparts were built in native style, not Roman, with gateways aligned with the routes from London, from Cirencester, and the two roads from Chichester and Winchester, which merged into one road outside the town.[14] The earthwork defences may have been erected to protect the town from attacks by the tribesmen of the Catuvellaunian king Caratacus, who had escaped after the first battles against the Romans and after his defeat had made for South Wales. There may have been a detachment of II Augusta based at Silchester for a few years from AD 43 or just afterwards, but this is not generally regarded as a military base to hold down the population. Rather it was a military detachment billeted conveniently in a pro-Roman town, probably with the intention of helping to protect it from Caratacus.

Another line of earthwork defences, known as the Outer Earthwork, was probably built around AD 68–70, though the date is far from certain and there are as yet no other similar fortifications of this period at any other Romano British town, except perhaps for Winchester, where a line of earthwork defences has been partially traced around the town, firmly dated by coin evidence to the reign of Nero.

Chichester, later to become the tribal capital of Noviomagus Reginorum (sometimes rendered as Noviomagus Regnorum, or Regnensium), may also have housed a contingent of legionary soldiers in the early years after the Roman invasion, as has been suggested for Silchester. The site may have been used as a military stores base for a while, possibly for Vespasian's army as he moved westwards. By the middle of the AD 50s civilian industries had started to develop, producing pottery and bronze and enamel work.[15] An inscription, found in two pieces in 1740, is now lost, but fortunately it was described and drawn at the time of discovery.[16] It probably formed the base of a statue that has also been lost. It records a dedication to the Emperor Nero dated to around AD 58 to AD 60, in fulfilment of a vow. There is no mention of anyone's name, so it cannot be decided whether this inscription is personal or corporate, or military or civilian in character, but it does show that someone at Chichester subscribed to Roman-style dedications of loyalty to the Emperor at a very early date.

Winchester, later to be titled Venta Belgarum, was settled in the first two centuries BC, but seemingly abandoned until around AD 50. Although it was developed as a town by the end of the first century AD, its origins are obscure. As at Bath, a fort is expected but not found, and the earthwork ramparts that were discovered underlying the line of the later defences have been interpreted in the same light as the second circuit at Silchester, perhaps belonging to the period around AD 68–70 and erected at the time of the civil war between rival claimants for the Imperial throne. A coin of Nero was found in one of the post-holes of the timber south gate, which lends support to the suggestion that the defences belong to the uneasy circumstances after the suicide of Nero. The troops in Britain were restless and divided in their loyalties to Galba, Otho, Vitellius and Vespasian, so it is considered that the early town needed protection.[17] The earth defences at this early date can also be taken as a clear indication that the town was part of a client kingdom loyal to Rome, because otherwise the building of ramparts would have been forbidden.[18]

The Realm of Tiberius Claudius Togidubnus

These three early towns at Silchester, Chichester and Winchester all displayed signs of early development along Roman lines but they were clearly semi-independent of Roman government. They were not yet a part of the Roman province of Britannia, because these towns and their territories most probably constituted the kingdom of a British ruler called Tiberius Claudius Togidubnus, whose names indicate that he was a Briton who had been given Roman citizenship. The grant was probably by the Emperor Claudius, but since there is no firm evidence as to the date of the citizenship grant, it is also possible that it was Nero who enfranchised him. It was customary for newly created citizens to adopt the name of the person who had granted the privilege to them, so the British ruler took the Emperor's name. The first two components of this name, Tiberius Claudius, ought to indicate the Emperor Claudius, but they also formed part of Nero's names, so there is no definite solution to the problems of the authorship of the citizenship grant or the date when it was made.

Modern scholars generally use the form Togidubnus, though the name sometimes appears in older books as Cogidubnus, or Cogidumnus, or Togidumnus. The latter part of his name, -*dumno* or -*dubno* means 'powerful'.[19] The 'b' and 'm' sounds in Celtic languages could be interchangeable, and the transcription of British names into Latin forms was not always consistent. In most modern versions of Tacitus's works, the British king appears as Cogidubnus.

Togidubnus would have been a client king of the Romans, a modern term which is used to describe a common arrangement between the Roman government and native kings. The Roman term for this was *rex sociusque et amicus*, meaning 'king and friend and ally' of the Roman people, with no mention of the word 'client', which was reserved for the members of the entourage of important Roman statesmen. Client kings enjoyed the protection and support of Rome while keeping their own people in order and occasionally furnishing assistance in Roman wars.

After the excavation of the different phases of the magnificent Roman palace at Fishbourne, Togidubnus is almost inextricably associated with it, though in more recent years there has been a revision of this suggestion. The earlier version of Fishbourne may have been a Roman administrative centre rather than the palatial residence of the British client king, but the size and magnificence and the interior decoration of the early timber phase far outstrips anything else in the region, and it is close to Togidubnus's capital at Chichester.

Whether or not he lived at Fishbourne, Togidubnus was certainly a powerful British ruler, with jurisdiction over more than one tribe. Tacitus says that certain states were granted to Togidubnus as king: *quaedam civitates Togidumno regi donatae.*[20] This is reinforced by a reinterpretation of the famous inscription from Chichester,[21] which is damaged, but the latter part of his name survives at the left-hand edge of line 5. The inscription records the dedication of a temple to Neptune and Minerva. In the past, the damaged central section of the inscription describing Togidubnus was restored to read *Rex et legatus Augusti*, king and legate of the Emperor. To bestow this rank on Togidubnus would have been an extremely unusual gesture, indeed for any British chief, or any other native ruler inside or outside any other province. Nothing along these lines has ever been found to support the idea that the Romans bestowed such power on a native ruler. More recently the damaged line has been reinterpreted, suggesting with good reason that the text should read *Rex Magnus* or great king.[22] This was a title bestowed by the Romans on native client kings who ruled over more than one tribe or political group. Togidubnus therefore probably governed several tribes of south Britain, in alliance with Rome, just as Tacitus says.

The question has been raised, but no answers have yet come to light, as to the date when Togidubnus was awarded these different states. He may have been granted all of them at the same time, when he was enfranchised, perhaps as early as AD 43, or a little later after the invasion. Alternatively he may have acquired the towns gradually as his territory expanded, perhaps Chichester first because it seems to have been his capital and it is close to Fishbourne, then Silchester when the Catuvellaunian domination was ended, and finally Winchester. Any permutation of these theories is possible.

It is certain that one of the tribes under the rule of Togidubnus was the Atrebates, whose erstwhile chief Verica, or Berikos, had been forced to appeal to Claudius for help, and was therefore indirectly responsible for the Roman conquest. Though the invasion was ostensibly undertaken on Verica's behalf, no-one knows what happened to him, or whether he was reinstated, even temporarily, as ruler of the Atrebates. Togidubnus may have been a distant relative, or one of Verica's descendants, or at any rate his appointed successor. As ruler of a wide area including Chichester, Silchester and Winchester, it is just possible that Togidubnus may have been involved in the foundation of Aquae Sulis.

3

BATH BEGINS

A lot was happening in Roman Britain in the AD 70s, when the first Roman baths and temples were built at Aquae Sulis. The decade after the rebellion of Boudicca was one of slow recovery rather than continual advance and conquest. The two Roman senators, who were appointed as governors of Britain after the recall of Suetonius Paullinus, were Publius Petronius Turpilianus from AD 61 to 63, and Trebellius Maximus from AD 63 to 69. These men were not fire-eating generals. Though they had seen some military service, they had more experience with civilian and legal affairs, and their terms of office in Britain were uneventful, giving Tacitus the opportunity to sneer at their lack of achievement compared to other generals. For the last years of Nero's reign, it seems that pacification was the order of the day, with no overt Roman Imperial intention to continue with the subjugation of the tribes, moving into hitherto unconquered territories and annexing them.

At some time, according to Suetonius, who unfortunately does not provide a specific date, it was said that Nero considered giving up the province of Britain altogether.[1] This may refer to an earlier episode when, after five years in Britain, the governor Didius Gallus had not lived up to expectations, and the conquest of Britain was going nowhere, but equally it could be that Nero became very discouraged after the rebellion of Boudicca, when there had been so many losses among the legions and auxiliaries, and three major towns had been destroyed.[2] Whatever the date of Nero's alleged wish to abandon Britain, Suetonius says that he did not do so because it would dishonour his father, referring to his predecessor Claudius, the conqueror of Britain. It is more likely that Nero changed his mind because it was pointed out to him that there would be a loss of revenue. This advice was probably given by elite Romans at Nero's court who feared that if the army withdrew from Britain they would not be able to recoup their loans to various British leaders, losing the capital and also the interest levied on the loans.

The civil war of AD 69 also stifled any dynamic military activity in the province of Britannia. The troops were divided among themselves, and the legate of Legio XX, Roscius Coelius, fomented trouble that kept Trebellius fully occupied. The provincial army was reduced in size from four legions to three, when one of the legions was removed to fight in the civil war. This was Legio XIV Gemina, which was taken to Italy, sent back to Britain, and then removed again, this time for good. When Vespasian finally emerged as victorious sole Emperor there was a revolt immediately afterwards by the Batavians on the Rhine. When this had been suppressed, Roman Imperial attention could be devoted once again to Britain. Between AD 71 and AD 83 or 84, three dynamic and trusted governors were sent out: Petillius Cerialis, who subdued the north of England and part of lowland Scotland; Sextus Julius Frontinus, who completed the conquest of Wales; and Gnaeus Julius Agricola, who brought Scotland within the Empire, though it was held for only a short time.

The important point for a history of Bath is that the south became less intensively occupied by the military and was gradually turned over to civilian development. There would probably not have been a complete withdrawal of all troops, because the Roman army performed many tasks other than just fighting and conquering. The soldiers carried out the functions of many of the uniformed officials of our own day, such as police, customs officials, also acting as guards for various purposes, especially for any permitted native gatherings, such as trading centres and markets. There would be a continual presence of military messengers, soldiers gathering supplies of food and clothing, collecting taxes and even soldiers on leave, or skulking as deserters or those who had gone AWOL. Once the Romans arrived, the Bath area, like all others, would never be entirely free of soldiers.

All over the new province of Britannia, during the reigns of the three Flavian Emperors from AD 69 to 96, there was a detectable increase in town development, new building or rebuilding, and the development of civic amenities. Excavations at numerous sites in southern Britain have revealed evidence that this period was one of increasing prosperity and urbanisation, when the towns that had been destroyed in the rebellion of Boudicca, Londinium (London), Camulodunum (Colchester) and Verulamium (St Albans), began to prosper again, and new towns were being established. Many Roman monumental buildings started to appear in towns all over southern Britain, with the construction of forum and basilica complexes, market places, temples and bathing establishments, as well as shops and houses. The foundation and development of Bath belongs in this context.

The Development of Romano-British Towns in the South-West

As the Romans extended their control over Wales, the north of England and then Scotland, troop numbers thinned out in the south and south-west. With a reduced Roman military presence, the sites where forts had been erected were often given up to the civilian population, if the tribal leaders so desired. It was standard practice all over the growing Empire for the civilians to move in when the soldiers moved out.

Cities and towns in the Roman Empire were graded in status. It is worth enumerating and describing them, since it will be seen that on present knowledge, Aquae Sulis does not readily slot into any of the categories and so remains an anomaly. The *coloniae* were the highest-grade towns. In Britain there were eventually four, possibly five, *coloniae*. The earliest was at Colchester (Camulodunum, also called Colonia Claudia Victricensis), then two more were created at Gloucester (Glevum, or Colonia Nervia Glevensium) and Lincoln (Lindum, or Colonia Domitiana Lindensium), where the first settlers were legionary veterans. In the third century the civilian town at York which had grown up on the opposite side of the River Ouse to the legionary fortress, was raised to colonial status by Severus or possibly by his son Caracalla. The *colonia* at York is to be distinguished from the *canabae* where civilians had settled around the fortress.

The status of London is not certain. Tacitus specifically states that it was not a *colonia* but an important and very busy settlement for traders,[3] but it seems that it was also the provincial headquarters for the governor and the finance officials, and although definite evidence is lacking, it is thought that London did eventually become a fourth *colonia*. In the late Roman period London acquired a new title of Augusta, which supports the theory that its status was elevated.

The next grade in town status was the *municipium*, which was a self-governing chartered town, but not quite as prestigious as a *colonia*. In a *municipium* local laws could remain in force, whereas a *colonia* was subject to Roman law.[4] Only one definite example of a *municipium* is known so far in Britain, at Verulamium, modern St Albans, where there had been a British centre labelled by the Romans as an *oppidum*, like the early native settlements in Gaul. In its formative years, London may have been a *municipium*.[5] The men who had served a term as the chief magistrates of a *municipium* usually received Roman citizenship, with all the legal rights and privileges that this entailed. Roman citizenship did not mean that the person so endowed hailed from Rome. Very early in the history of the Roman Empire, a means had evolved of granting citizenship to individuals or communities without the necessity of living in the city.

Since the Britons had little or no tradition of town life as the Romans understood it, other towns of lesser grade, varying in size and importance, had to be built from the ground up, sometimes on the sites of existing Iron Age settlements as at Camulodunum (Colchester) and Verulamium (St Albans), sometimes on virgin sites, and more often where forts had been given up, one of the most famous being the conversion of the legionary base at Wroxeter into a fairly large and prosperous town.

It was once thought that this sort of urbanisation was more or less organised if not made compulsory by the Roman authorities, but nowadays after work by Martin Millett[6] it is suggested that any such development was left to civilian initiative, possibly aided and encouraged by the Romans, but Romanisation was not necessarily an ideology forced onto a reluctant population.

If it is correct to assume that the Romans relied on local initiative rather coercion, then the development of towns, industries and villas in Roman Britain demonstrates that the resident population – of the southern parts of the island, at least – readily embraced the Roman way of life. There may have been many immigrants and settlers of varied nationality, most of them already Romanised, who formed the initial population, but the native tribes also remained in evidence, rather than being overwhelmed and obliterated. Even the Iceni survived after the Boudiccan rebellion had been suppressed, though the Roman town that was established for them at Caistor-by-Norwich (Venta Icenorum) was not much more than a backwater for a long time, very slow to flourish, and its development was never comparable to other more prosperous towns. The inhabitants of the southern half of Britain started to build towns very early in the Roman occupation, and underneath many Roman villas archaeologists have frequently found the remains of a British-style roundhouse. At one time it may have been considered that Roman settlers had ousted the British natives in the same way that the Normans took over Saxon settlements, but nowadays it is thought that this common occurrence of native farms being replaced with Roman villas represents a desire for expansion and improvement on the part of the Britons.

The northern tribes of the Pennine uplands and beyond did not adopt Roman ways as readily as their southern neighbours did, but continued to live in Iron Age roundhouses, trading readily enough with the Romans without converting their dwellings to Roman styles. Villa sites are few and far between in the north, though this may simply represent lack of excavation. More recently a few such villa sites have been discovered, but in general the north was not Romanised to the same degree as the south.

Civitas Capitals

Most of the new towns of Roman Britain were tribal centres, known in modern archaeological and historical literature as *civitas* capitals, indicating that they were the administrative centres for the tribes, or *civitates,* which could be translated as 'states'.

Unlike Londinium (London), Camulodunum (Colchester) and Verulamium (St Albans), the tribal capitals usually had double names, describing the town and also the tribe to which they belonged, as for instance the town mentioned above, Venta Icenorum, meaning Venta of the Iceni. The tribe would be self-governing as far as possible within the framework of Roman provincial government. There would be a governing body called the *ordo*, sometimes referred to in English as the council or the senate. There was a property qualification for membership of the *ordo*, which normally consisted of 100 decurions, though this number may not have applied in all towns, especially the smaller ones. The headquarters was based in the *civitas* capital and there would be a small body of annually elected magistrates, whose functions were organised on Roman lines, the chief magistrates being the *duoviri iuridicundo*, who held legal and administrative responsibilities. The town council was responsible for collecting the taxes due to the Roman government and would control the surrounding territory and the rural inhabitants belonging to the tribe. The majority of the population would remain as *peregrini*, or non-Roman citizens; the word actually means 'foreigners'. The men who had served as chief magistrates would sometimes receive Roman citizenship like those of a *municipium*.

The presence of a forum and basilica complex within a town usually indicates that this was where the administrative functions of the tribe were carried out, in a part of the building complex, designated as the *curia*. In the later Empire the members of the *ordo* were labelled *curiales*. Each tribe would have its designated territory all around the *civitas* capital, and sometimes if the territory was very extensive, it is possible that there was more than one centre where administrative, legal and religious procedures were performed. Local tribal government was always subordinated to Roman provincial government exercised by the governor and his staff.

Was Togidubnus the Founder of Bath?

A fragment of an inscription found in the Roman baths at some unknown date provides the most important clue to the date of the foundation of the spa town. This inscription[7] was not recognised for what it was until 1903, when the few letters visible on it were interpreted as 'VES. VII. CO.', referring to the seventh consulship of the Emperor Vespasian, which he held in AD 76. This may refer to the date when the first foundation stones were laid, or more probably the inscription was erected when the buildings were finished, dedicated, and ceremonially opened. A date of AD 76 accords well with the earliest detectable Roman building work at Bath, which belongs to the middle of the AD 70s, when the temple of Sulis Minerva was erected and the most important of the hot springs was surrounded by an embanked wall to convert it into a pool. The whole project was carried out on classical Roman lines, and presumably cost money. The initiative derived either from Roman officials, or from a native or natives with Roman support, but no-one knows whose idea it was to create a religious complex around the hot springs.

The Alexandrian author of a geographical treatise, Claudius Ptolemaeus, more familiarly known as Ptolemy, says in his *Geography* that Aquae Sulis was a *polis* (Greek for city or town) of the tribe of the Belgae, whose *civitas* capital was Venta Belgarum, modern Winchester.[8] Ptolemy's work was compiled in the latter half of the second century, using the reports of other authors who had travelled to places in the world as it was then known. In this respect he acknowledges his debt to an author called Marinus of Tyre, but unfortunately the work of this individual is lost and nothing else is known about him, though it may have been Marinus who gathered information about Britain. It is thought that the source or sources that Ptolemy used for the British sections derived from the first century, possibly as early as the reigns of Claudius or Nero, or at least no later than the reigns of the three Flavian Emperors, who reigned from AD 69 to 96.

Ptolemy's attribution of Aquae Sulis to the administrative area of Venta Belgarum is not accepted by all scholars.[9] It could be that there was a mistake in Ptolemy's sources, which he never questioned because he believed that the information was correct. If he had doubted his source, he could have checked by asking someone in the relevant Imperial administrative department in Rome, though since he worked in Alexandria it would have taken a little time to receive a reply, and in any case the government of a small town with some hot springs in far-away Britannia would hardly have been of major concern to him in the first place.

There are arguments for and against the suggestion that Togidubnus was responsible for the foundation of Bath. Two factors support the theory. The native settlement at Winchester that would ultimately become the *civitas* capital of Venta Belgarum was most likely part of the composite realm of the British client king Tiberius Claudius Togidubnus, along with Chichester and Silchester. If Ptolemy was correct in assigning Aquae Sulis to the *civitas* capital of the Belgae, it endorses the suggestion that Togidubnus was responsible for the establishment of the temple and baths at Bath. A slightly more substantial piece of evidence, not dependent on the veracity or otherwise of Ptolemy, supports the idea. During the excavations of the 1980s, a fragment of what had been a monumental inscription was found, with the letters 'TI. CL. T...' possibly standing for Tiberius Claudius Togidubnus. The inscription may have been associated with the temple of Sulis Minerva, or possibly some other important building, and it may therefore record the driving force and possibly the financial support of Togidubnus in establishing the first buildings at Bath. Further evidence is necessary before this hypothesis can be proven, but it is not beyond the bounds of possibility. Another inscription[10] which may be relevant was found in 1861 when the extensions to the Mineral Water Hospital were being built. It was a fragment of fine, white marble which had been imported to Britain, and therefore represents someone with the necessary wealth to pay for it. The marble fragment has since been lost, despite a search for it in 1936 and again in 1951, but a drawing was made of it for an article published in the *Proceedings of the Somersetshire Archaeological and Natural History Society* in 1863. Only a small part of the first three lines survived, interpreted as 'DEAE S ...

TI.CL.T ... SOLLEN ... (or SOLLEM ...)'. The transcription is usually rendered as 'To the goddess Sulis, Tiberius Claudius, son of Tiberius, Sollem(nis)'. At the time when this fragment was found, it was thought that Cogidubnus was the correct version of Togidubnus's name, because that is how it appears in the versions of Tacitus's work handed down from copies made in the early medieval period. However, since Togidubnus is now thought to be the correct version of the name, and another fragment has been found more recently which possibly refers to Tiberius Claudius Togidubnus, this inscription found in the nineteenth century, not impossibly distant from the temple of Sulis Minerva and the Roman baths, carved on expensive marble, may belong to the same man. The first part of the name ought to indicate that whoever this person was, he had been given citizenship by the Emperor Claudius, or less likely by Nero, just as Togidubnus had been made a Roman citizen. The assumption that the letter 'T' at the end of the second line of the marble fragment would have been followed by 'F' for *filius*, standing for 'son of Tiberius', may be correct, indicating that whoever erected this inscription was the descendant of an enfranchised Roman citizen, but it cannot be substantiated unless a matching fragment is discovered. It is not known how long the original inscription would have been, so it cannot be established what it may have commemorated. The name Sollemnis does not occur in other places, and does not usually find its way into modern works on Roman Britain with any explanation as to who he might have been. In Latin, *sollemnis* means solemn, or ceremonial. There is a possibility that this lost fragment belongs to Togidubnus, who left a record that he had founded some building dedicated to Sulis with all due ceremonial, or carried out some function with solemnity.

A possible objection to Togidubnus as founder of Bath is that the precise date when building work started on the temple of Sulis Minerva and the baths is not known, except within the parameters of the later AD 70s and early 80s, nor is the age of Togidubnus himself when the religious complex and bathing establishment was planned. According to Tacitus,[11] Togidubnus remained loyal to Rome up to recent times, or 'within living memory' (*ad nostrum usque memoriam fidissimus mansit*), that is up to the later years of the first century, before Tacitus started his career as a historian. If Togidubnus was about twenty to thirty years old at the time of the conquest in AD 43 he would be in his early fifties or sixties when Bath was founded around AD 75, not an impossible age to instigate building projects. It may have been one of his last public acts before he died, since it is considered that his death probably occurred in the last years of the AD 70s. This would be consistent with Tacitus's statement that Togidubnus remained loyal up to the times that he and his contemporaries could remember. It is also consistent with the rebuilding of the Roman palace at Fishbourne, when around AD 75 to 80 a truly magnificent complex was built, dwarfing the previous, already magnificent, former dwelling, which fitted easily into one corner of the new version.[12] This may represent the changes that were made just after the death of Togidubnus when his palace was converted into an even more sumptuous residence, either for his descendants or for Roman governmental officials.

A further problem that could militate against the attribution of Bath to local government from Winchester is that the development of Winchester itself seems to lag behind that of Bath. A defensive earthen bank with timber gates was built at Winchester around AD 70, and a series of timber buildings, some with more than one phase, were erected inside the defences, but there was no Roman-style street-grid until around AD 90, and the forum dates only from about AD 100, over two decades after the foundation of the temple of Sulis Minerva and the baths at Bath. These factors do not necessarily disprove the theory that Togidubnus was the founder of Bath, since he was perfectly entitled to act independently within his own kingdom, erecting Roman-style buildings in any part of it, as long as his plans did not adversely affect the government of the province of Britannia. He could have organised the foundation of the new spa town of Aquae Sulis from a base in Silchester, or even from Winchester itself, even though the site did not yet possess a Roman-style forum and basilica. As suggested in the previous chapter, the presence of defences around Winchester dated to around AD 70, similar to those at Silchester but earlier than those of any other town, implies that the town was independent of Roman provincial government, thus supporting the idea that it was part of Togidubnus's kingdom. One of the reasons why Roman buildings did not make an early appearance at Winchester, comparable to those at Silchester for instance, is that Togidubnus may have obtained control of the town at a much later time than Silchester and Chichester, so by the early AD 70s he had not had sufficient time to embellish the place. At the time of the foundation of Bath around AD 75 it is highly likely that Venta Belgarum, perhaps under a different name, was in its nascent stages of development, still ruled by Togidubnus as a client king. As an independent ruler, he would not need to set up a Roman-style administrative system with a town council and annually elected magistrates in order to set in motion the foundation of a spa town in the lands which he governed. Rudimentary administrative functions could be operated for a couple of decades from Winchester without the benefit of a recognisable Roman forum and basilica. Alternatively if Togidubnus felt the need for such amenities in his government, he could have set up headquarters in Silchester, which is not so far away from Bath, and there was a timber forum and basilica there from at least AD 50, the earliest so far known in Britain.

On the basis of present knowledge it is perfectly feasible that in the later years of his life Togidubnus could have drawn up plans to develop the religious centre at Bath and started work on it. Only after his death would his kingdom, with the main towns of Silchester, Chichester and Winchester, be absorbed into the province. These towns would then be designated as *civitas* capitals for a tribe or specified group of people. Each town would be allocated its own territory, including any smaller towns and villages, with the boundaries clearly defined, and the responsibility of each town with regard to its territory would be set down at the time of its formation. In this case, Ptolemy was probably entirely correct in attributing Aquae Sulis to the *civitas* capital of the Belgae at Winchester, because that really was the situation when his source material was gathered. Whatever form his sources took, they were perhaps compiled in the later first century AD, just after the death of Togidubnus, and consequently on the cusp of the change from semi-independent client kingdom to full absorption into the province. At that point, the *civitas* capital of Venta Belgarum would still have been in its early stages of development and the extent of its administrative territories had probably only just been drawn up and not yet fully implemented.

Who Were the People Who Lived Around Bath?

All over the Roman Empire, client states usually retained their independence only while the favoured ruler still lived, and were not usually handed down to successors. After the death of Togidubnus, his kingdom was absorbed into Britannia. It was normal procedure for the Romans to take over the government of his kingdom, incorporate it fully into the Roman province and divide it up into smaller administrative groupings, each with its own *civitas* capital. After the death of Togidubnus in the late AD 70s the three main settlements of his kingdom were converted into *civitas* capitals, Silchester as Calleva Atrebatum, Chichester as Noviomagus Reg(i)norum, and Winchester as Venta Belgarum. From then onwards more building work along Roman lines was undertaken, regular street-grids were laid out, and public amenities increased.

Silchester was the most heavily Romanised settlement in Togidubnus's realm. Roman-style public buildings had been in existence here several years before the first comparable buildings appeared at Bath. Around AD 80 a new timber version of Silchester's forum was built, and a regular street-grid was drawn up.

Chichester may have been the administrative centre for the eastern parts of Togidubnus's kingdom, and had been used perhaps as a short-lived fort, then a stores base, then as an industrial centre. As a civilian settlement and *civitas* capital it was laid out on a regular street-grid from about AD 75, and towards the end of the second century, a forum and basilica and an amphitheatre were erected. The text of the damaged inscription recording Togidubnus as *Rex Magnus*,[13] also bearing the names of Neptune and Minerva and the word *templum*, reveals that before the death of Togidubnus a temple to these two deities was built somewhere in Roman Chichester, but its location has not yet been discovered. Outside the town boundaries, a cemetery was established for the deceased inhabitants from around AD 70.

The Romans reorganised the newly assimilated territories of Togidubnus's kingdom for political reasons, to simplify administration and control. Some of the new territories were probably settled by amalgamations of different groups of people. It has been argued that the inhabitants of Chichester, the new *civitas* capital called Noviomagus Reginorum, were originally members of several different small tribes which had formed part of the kingdom (*regnum* in Latin) of Togidubnus.[14] The name of these people is variously considered to be Regni, Regini, or Regnenses. There is no absolute certainty, since the tribal capital is not consistently named, appearing either as Noviomagus Reg(i)norum, or sometimes as Noviomagus Regnensium. Not all scholars agree with the derivation of the name from *regnum*, nor is there universal acceptance of the theory that the people were of diverse groupings.[15] It is also worth noting that no tribe called the Regni, or any of the variations of the name, has yet been attested before the *civitas* capital was founded.

It is debatable whether or not the territorial boundaries that were created by the Roman administrators respected those of the older tribal areas. Some scholars are of the opinion that on occasion the Romans ignored existing tribal boundaries for the sake of administrative convenience, especially in the cases where new groupings of people were amalgamated and given a new tribal centre.[16] On the other hand, it has been argued, on analogy with the Roman government of the Gallic provinces, that the

Roman administrators would utilise the tribal sub-divisions that were already in place rather than drawing up new boundaries.[17] However it was accomplished, whether by arbitrary means or by following traditional boundaries, the changes in tribal nomenclature and leadership simply continued the customary periodic re-groupings that had occurred among the Iron Age peoples, where smaller tribes were assimilated by larger ones and new names emerged for the new federations.

The development of Winchester was not as advanced as that of Chichester, and lagged far behind Silchester. Although it is generally agreed to have been part of the kingdom of Togidubnus, it is not certain when he acquired the territory. He may have been granted this additional territory at a later time than the areas around Silchester and Chichester. The fact that Winchester's Roman street-grid was not laid out until around AD 90, and its forum dates to about a decade later, probably represents the slower organisation of the resident population and an initial lack of cohesion. There is considerable uncertainty about the people who composed the new and probably artificial tribal grouping centred on Venta Belgarum. The name denotes broad ethnicity rather than a specific tribe, implying that the Romans created an entirely new administrative district for the purposes of local government.[18] It has long been noted that there is no archaeological or historical evidence for a properly organised Belgic state established in the area before the foundation of the *civitas* capital.[19] Possible solutions to this problem include the possibility that different people from smaller tribes were grouped together and renamed as Belgae, or the so-called Belgae may have been later immigrants purposely imported by the Romans, perhaps during the conquest or even after the death of Togidubnus.

Before the Roman conquest, the whole area around Winchester was probably originally settled by several smaller tribes, possibly all anti-Roman but otherwise not united, whose territory was taken over and deliberately resettled by people who were more tractable. If this sort of pacification had to be undertaken from the Roman conquest onwards, it may be the case that the area was not handed over to Togidubnus until it was considered safe, which in turn supports the theory that it was a later addition to Togidubnus's kingdom. Although the use of the tribal name Belgae is acknowledged as an artificial creation for the new *civitas* capital, it was not altogether an invention. Pottery studies indicate that a group or groups of Belgic pottery manufacturers followed the Roman army as the troops moved into the south-western areas of Britain.[20] Belgic pottery is found on many sites in the region around Winchester, but it does not constitute evidence for a Belgic state.

Geographically closer to Bath, at Cirencester, the fort there was abandoned in the AD 70s and a tribal capital was established, named Corinium Dobunnorum, or Corinium of the Dobunni. It was most likely the inhabitants of the *vicus* around the fort who moved into the new town at first. From probably modest beginnings, Corinium Dobunnorum was eventually to become the second largest town in Roman Britain, after London. The earliest known forum and basilica at Cirencester dates to the end of the first century AD and was built in stone, which may mean that there was a much earlier timber version built around AD 70 to 75 which needed to be replaced, or alternatively that the inhabitants were wealthier and more style-conscious than those of other towns and were determined that their town should appear to best advantage from the very start.

Since Ptolemy assigns the administration of Bath to Winchester, it precludes the possibility that the town council of Cirencester ever held any responsibility for the government of the religious centre and the hot springs and baths, so the connection between Cirencester and Bath may not have been very close in the initial stages. But as the tribal capital of the Dobunni grew in size, importance, and wealth, the relations between the two centres probably flourished, for instance a sculptor called Sulinus, son of Brucetus, who worked at Bath[21] was also active at Cirencester and may have had his workshop there.[22] The opportunities that were offered for trading, marketing and providing service industries at the religious and bathing establishments at Bath would not have gone unnoticed by the business communities of Cirencester.

Further afield, other *civitas* capitals were set up around the same time as those at Cirencester, Silchester, Chichester and Winchester. Dorchester in Devon became the centre for the Durotriges, called Durnovaria, but without the usual tribal name attached to it. Not much is known of the town itself, but in the decade AD 70 to 80, when Bath was in its early stages, the inhabitants of Durnovaria constructed an amphitheatre by re-using the ramparts of a nearby Neolithic earthwork, and an aqueduct with a timber-lined channel brought water to the town. This indicates that there was a population there to enjoy these amenities in the later first century.

The legionary base at Exeter was given up in the AD 70s, and the town became the centre for the Dumnonii, named Isca Dumnoniorum. The forum and basilica was begun about AD 75, like so many others in the south and south-west, but here this administrative complex was not a completely new foundation, since the legionary bath house was remodelled to provide it.

At Gloucester, at the time when the first buildings appeared at Bath, the legionary soldiers were still in occupation, though perhaps not for very long, till perhaps AD 90 or possibly a little earlier. When the fortress was given up, the civil settlement of the *colonia* was inhabited at first by veterans, using the old barracks. Its name was Glevum, the full title being Colonia Nervia (or Nerviana) Glevensium. The name of the Emperor Nerva included in the title is normally taken to mean that the colony was founded in his reign, which was very short, from AD 96 to 98, but it has also been suggested that the actual foundation dates back to the reign of Domitian, whose name may have been attached to the colony for legionary veterans at Lincoln. He was assassinated in 96, and died unloved by nearly everyone, except the soldiers, because he had given them a long overdue pay rise. His name was deleted from all monuments and therefore the colony's title may have been adjusted accordingly. Whatever the true date of Roman Gloucester, when the temple and baths were built at Bath, one of its nearest neighbours was still a military base.

The nearest potential clientèle for the religious centre and the bathing establishment at Bath included all those who were settled in the tribal capitals and the surrounding countryside, the people of the surrounding tribes, the Dobunni, the Dumnonii, the Durotriges, the Belgae, the Atrebates, the Regni, the agricultural workers and farmers, and all the people who gravitated to the towns, the decurions or town councillors belonging to the governing *ordo*, the shopkeepers, traders, builders, plumbers, lead miners, sculptors, stone carvers, pottery manufacturers and the like, who worked in and around the towns, and also soldiers from the bases that were still occupied or who were in the area on official business. Then eventually there would be the doctors, the oculists, the spiritual healers, the lawyers, the touts, the trinket sellers, food retailers and the tavern keepers. As a speculative economic and religious development, the enclosure and control of the hot springs at Bath probably looked like a safe bet.

Roman Bath in Context: Spa Baths and Conventional Baths

The first task before the major buildings could be started at Bath was the draining of the boggy ground and the enclosure of the main hot spring, since there was no point in erecting buildings in the marsh all around it. This preparation of the ground constituted a considerable engineering task, but the Romans already possessed long and wide-ranging experience and practice in architectural engineering, in particular water engineering. There were many other spas in the Roman Empire. At least twenty-nine of these were given double-barrelled Latin names beginning with Aquae, signifying the waters of somewhere or someone, and there were yet more spas situated in towns which did not use the Aquae prefix. There were two Aquae places in Britain, at Bath and at Buxton, the latter called Aquae Arnemetiae. Several of these spas all over the Roman world preceded Bath by many years. Aquae Sextiae, for example, was founded in 122 BC. It is now called Aix-en-Provence, the Aix element being derived from Aquae, as at other towns in France with the same prefix, and at Aachen, whose alternative name is Aix-la-Chapelle.

Aquae Sextiae has similar origins to Bath in that it was an important military and political base as well as a spa. It was established in the plain below the Gallic *oppidum* of Entremont, so its first function was to control the area and keep the local population in order, much as the postulated fort at Bath would have served to protect the routes and the crossing of the River Avon. The military function of Aquae Sextiae dictated that it should be in a generally convenient location close to the *oppidum*, but the specific location of the town depended on the spot where the hot springs emerged.

Spa towns in the Roman Empire, then as now, consisted of two main kinds. The medicinal and healing qualities of waters bearing specific minerals, most commonly sulphur, were well appreciated, but not all of these derived from hot springs. Waters bearing minerals but not heat could be piped to a location that best suited the foundation of bathing establishments. The mineral content would not be lost if the water was made to travel some distance, but hot springs could not be piped for any distance without losing the beneficial heat, so the waters had to be harnessed *in situ*, as at Bath.

The baths of a spa should be distinguished from the conventional bathing establishments. The spa baths were obviously designed to cater for the healing and medicinal needs of the clientèle, with arrangements for partial or total immersion, and perhaps for taking the waters in the modern sense of consuming it, though it is far from certain if the Romans drank the waters at Bath or at any of their other spas. The prime purpose of the conventional baths was for cleansing procedures. Water had to be brought in and heated artificially by a boiler or a series of boilers. The larger bathing establishments were usually supplied by one or more aqueducts, but smaller ones may have a system of bucket chains or a compartment waterwheel powered by humans to raise the water to a tank on the roof, where a sufficient head of water could be obtained to keep the baths supplied. The hot water tanks would need filling all the time and there may have been showers and fountains as well. When an aqueduct was available the water was usually directed to a distribution tank, or tanks, which kept the other areas supplied.

Bathing procedure was to enter via the entrance hall, or *apodyterium*, where clothes were left behind, then to move into the warm room, the *tepidarium*, heated to about 25 degrees centigrade, and from there into the hot room, the *caldarium*, where the water providing steam came in at about 40 degrees centigrade, somewhat cooler than the waters of Bath. In addition to the boiler system for heating the water in tanks, a furnace or a series of them, depending on the size of the establishment, was required to heat the hot and warm rooms. Heat was piped under the floors, which were raised on pillars made of stone or stacked tiles to allow the hot air to circulate. This under-floor heating system is known as a hypocaust. Hollow box-flue tiles could be set inside the walls to carry the heat up the sides of the room. It was an efficient system, and the floors in a centrally heated private house could be too hot for bare feet. There is a story that an unfortunate landowner in Italy was set upon by his slaves, who threw him onto the heated floor to see if he was still alive, but he gritted his teeth and emerged intact but with burns.

The object of the progression from the warm room to the hot room was to induce perspiration. The bathers rubbed themselves with oil, and scraped off the oil and sweat together, using a curved metal instrument called a strigil. Next the bather could proceed back into the warm room, the *tepidarium*, and finally into the cold room, the *frigidarium*, where there was usually a cold plunge. The modern conception of Roman baths is that the plunge baths could be horrendously filthy, and various ancient authors are cited to illustrate these horrors, especially medical treatises which report the fact that if you had an open wound it was best not to enter these pools. On the other hand, the plumbing and drainage systems of Roman baths have not been studied in as much depth as the architecture, so it is not possible to state categorically that the baths were never drained or that the water was not regularly changed. The water presumably flowed out from the baths as well as in, and in one or two cases it is clear that after it had flowed through the bathing areas, the water that would otherwise have gone to waste was used to flush the communal public toilets that were usually attached to the baths, a purpose for which clean water was not absolutely necessary. Very few Roman bathing establishments have yielded evidence of how the water was used and the course that it followed through the baths, but Bath is an exception, and even though the areas investigated do not constitute the whole of the precincts around the baths, enough has been gleaned to be able to say how they worked.

The major baths, especially those in Rome like the baths of Trajan, Caracalla and Diocletian, were enormous complexes covering several acres. They were the leisure centres of their day, involving not just a method of washing and hygiene, but also areas dedicated to recreational pursuits such as athletics, gaming, gambling and reading. Several baths had libraries attached to them. Most of the larger establishments also possessed swimming pools, *natationes*, in addition to the plunge baths which operated as part of the cleansing process.

At Bath, both types of bathing establishments were provided. The hot springs were siphoned off into the Great Bath, where people could immerse themselves in the healing waters, and at the western end of the whole complex there was a conventional bath with the hot room, warm room and cold room. It has been pointed out that photographs of the large bath surrounded by its walls is often used to illustrate not just the town of Roman Bath, but Roman baths in general, which is not strictly accurate.

The Buildings of the First Century AD at Bath

The temple of Sulis Minerva and the baths were obviously founded by someone with foresight and vision, either by Togidubnus, or by a Roman official, perhaps even the governor of Roman Britain, or at least by a combination of local initiative and Roman encouragement. Neither the founder nor the builders are known, but the first structures at Bath are very sophisticated, they are classical in design rather than native Romano-British, and the stonework is among the best in the province. In many cases where civilian buildings appear in a town with this level of sophistication it is suggested that perhaps military stonemasons were involved, but around AD 75 when Bath was founded, the soldiers were mostly involved in campaigns in the north or in Wales, in a province that was not yet fully pacified, so perhaps it is unlikely that military architects were assigned to the project. Since some of the work has parallels in Gaul, it is possible that Gallic builders and especially sculptors may have been brought to Britain to start the work at Bath. One day an inscription or two might turn up to clarify matters. When John Leland visited Bath in the sixteenth century, impressive numbers of sculptures and inscriptions were visible in the walls on two sides of the city, from the south gate via the west gate right round to the north gate, having been re-used to create the defences of the later Roman period. Some of them may be buried somewhere underneath more modern buildings, and names and maybe dates might be carved on them. One can but dream.

The current state of knowledge about the first buildings at Bath derives from several excavations conducted over the last 250 years, culminating in those by Professor Barry Cunliffe, whose excavation reports described the more recent findings and also tied all the loose ends together from previous investigations by antiquarians and historians to provide a coherent account of the development of Roman Bath. Since this process involves much guesswork, it is also freely acknowledged that new finds could augment, amend or drastically alter the current state of knowledge about the spa town.

The Enclosure of the Sacred Spring

The main reason why the baths and temples were erected at Bath was the existence of the hot springs, and the location of all the buildings connected with the waters, including the temple of Sulis Minerva and the other religious establishments, the spa baths, and the conventional baths, was entirely dependent on the site where the waters flowed from the earth. None of the buildings could be founded in the vicinity of the spring until the marshy areas all around it had been properly dried out, so the first task was the provision of drainage at the hot springs to run off excess water, which would serve to keep the surroundings dry, and also allow the builders access to the vent. The enormous drain that the Romans built, large enough for people to walk through without hitting their heads on the arched vault, is still *in situ*. It is built of stone, with a rectangular gully at the bottom, lined with wood, some of which was preserved. It speaks volumes for the quality of Roman building techniques that 2,000 years later it has been restored and still functions as it was meant to, leading wastewater away from the modern baths. Nowadays the channel connects with the main sewer system, which dates from medieval times, but in Roman times the drain probably led straight into the River Avon.

The enclosure of the spring began with a circuit of oak piles driven into the earth around the spring, tightly packed together and arranged in a rough oval. This arrangement is similar to the foundations of buildings in Venice, where oak piles were used to provide a building platform. Oak is the best timber for this purpose because of its resistance to rot while set in the water. A gap was left in the circuit of oak piles around the spring, to marry up with the drain outlet, so that excess water could be run off and work could continue with the enclosure. A trench was dug all around the outside of the oak piles and a raft of timber piles placed at the bottom to provide a foundation for the stone wall that eventually ran all round the spring, projecting up to 2 metres above the ring of oak piles. This wall, like the ring of oak piles, had a square gap in it, deliberately set at the level of the pool, facing the mouth of the drain, where the water flowed out while building work was still going on.

During the archaeological excavation of the pool around the sacred spring, it was discovered that the Romans had not skimped on the waterproof lining. First, clay was used to seal off the tops of the oak piles. Then on top of this the pool was lined with massive sheets of lead, weighing almost half a ton, 1 centimetre thick and some 2.4 metres by 1.8 metres in size.[23] This lavish usage supports the statement of Pliny[24] that there was no shortage of lead in

Roman Britain. The Charterhouse mines not far from Bath most likely supplied the lead. Perhaps entrepreneurs such as Gaius Nipius Ascanius made a fortune, but it is not certain if private individuals were still in charge of the mines, since evidence suggests that the Emperor Vespasian had taken over the lead workings in Flintshire by the time that Bath was founded. He had possibly commandeered all the mines in Britain. He was, after all, short of cash. On his accession in AD 69 he had startled the Senate by explaining how many millions of sesterces were needed to shore up the treasury. If all mines were under Imperial control, then plans for the use of lead in the buildings of Bath would have been passed upwards via the governmental hierarchy to the Emperor himself.

The lead sheets lining the pool were carefully joined together by overlapping the vertical edges and sealing them by burning. At the bottom the lead was bent outwards to make a footing which was then covered with waterproof concrete, a most useful invention of the Romans, and sealed with a layer of tiles. At the top of the surrounding wall the lead sheets were bent over so there would be no seepage into the fabric of the wall.

When the lining of the pool was in place, the gap in the wall facing the drain was filled in and the pool was allowed to fill up with water. From the top of the pool the hot water could be channelled into the Great Bath. The water was not simply left to bubble up unattended. The engineers had realised in advance that the flow of water was not regulated or steady, and it was not just water that came up from the springs but also mud, sand and silt. There was a danger that this would block up the channels if it was allowed to accumulate. This is why the water was delivered into the Great Bath from the elevated top of the pool, so the mud had a chance to settle to the bottom before supplying the bath.

Provision had also been made for periodic cleaning out of the mud by means of a sluice, which had already been built into the stone wall above the original gap facing the drain. It had presumably always been the intention that this lower gap was a temporary provision only and it was to be blocked up when the work was finished. The sluice was also part of the original design, set there deliberately and with considerable foresight by the water engineers, rather than as a later solution to an unforeseen problem that arose after the springs had flowed for some time. It is not certain exactly how the system worked, but it is clear that when the mud had built up in the pool enclosing the spring, the sluice could be opened and the waters of the hot spring could be used to flush all the detritus away down the main drain, which had been built on a large enough scale to cope with such a periodic flow of mud. Perhaps the baths authorities, whoever they were, closed the Great Bath to customers while this was done, hopefully announcing their decision some days before.

In its first Roman version the spring was not roofed over, leaving it, apart from the enclosure wall, just as it had always been in pre-Roman times, an open-air, sacred site. To the south of it, the baths were constructed utilising the constant hot water, and surrounding the pool on the north, west and east sides the temple precincts were built, with the altar just to the north within sight of the pool, and the temple of Sulis Minerva to the north-east.

The Baths

The bath complex at Bath was used for at least three centuries, possibly for 350 years, surviving into the early fifth century when the Roman era finally ended. During this long time-span the buildings were altered, repaired and enlarged, so the earliest version of the baths is difficult to discern. It should hardly be surprising that apart from the inscription mentioning Vespasian's seventh consulship, dated to AD 76, no further precise information was obtained to establish the date of the first bath complex. The finds included a few pieces of pottery dating to the late first and early second centuries. However, on analogy with the way in which other towns were developing in Roman Britain towards the end of the first century AD, the monumental temple and baths of Aquae Sulis do not appear out of place. There was a detectable surge of building work in southern areas of the province at this period, creating new civilian settlements, either from virgin soil or on sites recently given up by the army, and embellishing them with forum and basilica complexes, temples and baths. As a religious centre and spa town, Bath may have been a little unusual but it fits into the context of development elsewhere. People were certainly visiting the place in the late first century AD and setting up inscriptions, which strongly suggests that there were buildings there and baths to visit, rather than a sacred hot spring in the open air, approached by a causeway across a sticky marsh.[25]

The baths were erected on an east–west alignment, south of the sacred spring and the temple of Sulis Minerva. The largest space was taken up by the Great Bath and two smaller ones to its east, while at the western end there was a conventional bath suite, with a series of rooms that have been identified as *frigidarium*, *tepidarium* and *caldarium*. The south-west corner of this conventional bath building is largely unknown because modern buildings obscure it, but it is suggested that the entrance hall or *apodyterium* would have been sited here. On the current plan, there is sufficient space for another room, almost square, in the angle between the *caldarium* and the southern end of the hall, or *frigidarium*, which runs north to south across the western end of the great Bath. This hall projects beyond the Great Bath at its southern end, and joins onto the enclosure wall of the spring on its northern side. Three large windows pierced this northern side, allowing bathers to view the spring itself.

Running eastwards from the long side of the conventional baths there is the Great Bath, fed by the hot springs. This is the most important section of the bath complex that is still visible today, though obviously much altered. Visitors who wanted to immerse themselves in the hot spring water came into the Great Bath through the hall or *frigidarium* of the conventional baths, crossing it diagonally from the entrance at the south-west corner. At the opposite corner of the *frigidarium*, the visitor would then turn right to enter the northern aisle of the Great Bath, following the path of the hot water piped under the floor from the spring.

Around all four sides of the Great Bath, long sides on the north and south, short sides on the east and west, there was a continuous arcade, so it was possible to walk around the bath itself on a fine paved floor made of limestone slabs, many of which are still visible. On the inside edge where the water lay, the aisles were flanked by arches supported on pillars, and the outside walls each had three symmetrical recesses, or *exedrae*, the central one square, and the outer ones semi-circular. These would provide niches for bathers to stand or sit. Drainage channels in the aisle floors delivered any water that splashed from the large pool, or dripped from bathers getting out of it, back into the Great Bath.

The Great Bath measured 24 metres by 12 metres, and its floor was 1.5 metres below the level of the aisles. All four sides of the bath were built as a series of four steps, quite steep, leading down into the water. The whole bath, including the steps, was originally lined with lead sheeting, measuring 3 metres by 1.5 metres, and 1 centimetre thick. The lead on the steps has disappeared. It is estimated that the whole lead lining would have weighed 86,000 kilograms.[26]

Moving further eastwards from the Great Bath, oriented across its narrow end with their longer sides on the east and west, there were two other swimming baths, one found in 1755, now called the Lucas Bath, and another slightly narrower one discovered in 1923 but not fully excavated. They were graded in size and perhaps also in the temperature of the water, being supplied via a channel from the Great Bath into the Lucas Bath, and another channel ran from the Lucas Bath into the so-called 1923 bath, so there was probably a gradual cooling as the water travelled through three sets of baths. Finally the water drained out of the south-east corner of the bathing complex.

The superstructure of the baths cannot be known in detail, especially since alterations were made throughout the three and a half centuries of the life of the building. Enough remnants of the foundations and the columns around the Great Bath have been revealed for archaeologists to reconstruct the probable appearance of the whole building from the ground plan. The central part, over the Great Bath, the Lucas Bath and the 1923 bath probably projected above the side aisles like a church building, with large windows in the upper storey to let in light. There is still uncertainty as to how the roof was constructed, or even if the first phase of the Great Bath was roofed at all. Analogy with other well-preserved bathing complexes, in particular the various baths at Pompeii, and the Hunting Baths preserved almost intact at Leptis Magna in modern Libya, suggests that the commonest roof types consisted of a concrete vault rather than a timber covering, which would have rotted away in the constant steamy environment. The rounded vault was often visible from the outside, as at Leptis, often left with its concrete covering and no other adornment.

Despite the need for a vaulted roof over the baths, it is thought that the first version of the roof of the bath complex at Bath, in the first century AD, may have taken the form of a pitched tiled roof, supported on timbers, with similar arrangements for the lower roofs covering the aisles and the *exedrae*. If there was such a roof, it would not have lasted for very long, no matter how well the wood had been seasoned, and so it was probably replaced in the second century by a concrete vault. Since Bath enjoyed or endured the somewhat damp British climate, the vault may have been covered by a tiled roof to run off the rain water.[27]

If there were any statues or other decorations around the inside or the outside of the late-first-century walls of the Great Bath, its satellite baths to the east, and the conventional baths to the west, they have all disappeared. On the north side of the Great Bath, in front of the central squared recess, there was a fountain. Even if it was a plain, unadorned building in its first phase, the baths complex was still a monumental edifice, very well built on classic Roman lines. No-one who saw it for the first time could have been in any doubt that a new era had dawned.

The Temple of Sulis Minerva

The number of inscriptions dedicated to Sulis Minerva at Bath certifies that the temple is correctly attributed to these two deities. The temple is of enormous importance for Romano-British archaeology, because the excavated remains serve to determine what it looked like. Elsewhere in the Roman Empire, there are some temples that are still intact, like the Maison Carrée in Nimes, or the so-called temple of Fortuna Virilis in Rome. In some cases enough of the temple façade has been preserved to show all the columns and the pediment, like the church of Santa Maria Sopra Minerva in Assisi. As the name of the church demonstrates, visitors enter a Christian church dedicated to Santa Maria by going up the Roman steps and on through the entrance of the temple dedicated to the goddess Minerva. For Roman Britain, most temples are known only through literary references, inscriptions, or archaeological discovery of the battered remains of the foundations. The preservation of any further architectural details is extremely rare. It cannot be emphasised too strongly that the appearance of no other temple in Roman Britain can be so well illustrated as the temple of Sulis Minerva.

When the Pump Room was built at the end of the eighteenth century, large sections of the temple pediment were found, including its central sculpture – variously called the Gorgon's head, Neptune or Oceanus – and held to represent the goddess, or in view of its masculine appearance, the god, Sulis. These remains were found together with fragments of the flanking sculptures and parts of the decorated cornice.

The temple is also important because classical Roman temples were not as common in Britain as the Romano-Celtic temples, whose label derives from the fact that they were widely distributed in Gaul as well as Britain. These were generally simpler affairs than classical temples, with a central rectangular or square interior projecting above a larger outer circuit of walls which enclosed what is usually interpreted as an ambulatory. At the Roman town of Caerwent in South Wales, visitors can see the ground plan of an example of this type of Romano-Celtic temple, clearly laid out in one of the excavated areas, together with display boards showing its probable external appearance.

There was a major classical Roman temple built at Colchester. Its foundation date is not known, but it was probably started as soon as possible after the Romans established themselves at Colchester. It was dedicated to the Emperor Claudius, though it is a subject of debate as to whether was dedicated to the Emperor as a living god in human form, or whether it was first dedicated to his *genius*, or spirit, and then to the divine Claudius after his death and deification. The temple is now completely sealed by the massive Norman castle built by William the Conqueror, who used the ruins of the temple podium and its vaults as the foundation of the castle. This temple was always well known from a famous literary reference. Tacitus[28] records that the temple was hated by the Britons as a symbol of oppression, and how the veterans of Legio XX tried to take refuge there as the warriors of Boudicca sacked Colchester. They were eventually overwhelmed and slaughtered. No-one knows whether the temple had been completed or whether it simply had walls that the veterans could defend, but in any case it would have to be rebuilt after AD 60. The literary reference of Tacitus was only verified in the 1920s when an investigation of the vaults underneath the castle revealed that they were part of a separate, earlier building, and did not belong to the Norman work, except as a firm foundation for a massive structure that was larger than the White Tower of London.[29]

Other classical Roman temples are known at London and Wroxeter, and also at York, where remains were found in 1989. Some of the temples at Corbridge may also have been classical in style and function, and it is feasible that the larger towns in Roman Britain such as Cirencester also held classical temples, but as yet there is no evidence for such buildings. At Chichester, the inscription[30] labelling Togidubnus as *Rex Magnus* shows that he authorised the building of a temple to Neptune and Minerva, financed by the guild of smiths (*collegium fabrorum*). The site is not known, and there is nothing to prove that it was classical in style rather than Romano-Celtic, but the fact that Togidubnus was granted citizenship and fully embraced the Roman away of life, coupled with his probable association with Fishbourne, and his possible association with Bath, suggest that the Chichester temple of Neptune and Minerva may have been similar to the temple of Sulis Minerva at Bath.

The paucity of actual remains of classical temples in Roman Britain demonstrates the supreme importance of the temple at Bath. The broken pieces of the pediment and parts of a few columns may not look so imposing at first sight, but until remains of a similar classical temple turn up in one of the other Romano-British towns, they are unique.

Most of the remains of the temple of Sulis Minerva lie underneath the modern Stall Street. It faced east, standing on a podium raised about 1.5 metres above ground level, and approached by a flight of steps leading to the eastern façade. The reconstruction of the pediment as seen in the Roman Baths Museum gives an idea of its dimensions, and judging by these measurements, there were probably four columns in the façade, fluted in the Corinthian style with leafy capitals, one of which was found in 1790 along with broken sections of the columns.[31] The appearance of the rest of the temple is not known. Like other classical temples it would have been rectangular, the longer sides stretching to the west for about 14 metres, and the façade and the rear probably measured about 9 metres.[32] The height of the columns is not established, but they were probably about 8 metres or 9 metres tall. The longer sides may have been built in plain blocks of stone, or alternatively there may have been a row of engaged columns, like pilaster buttresses, all around three sides of the temple. Some of the columns found in the eighteenth century had been hollowed out, which suggested that they had originally been flat-backed and may have been used as half-columns on the outside of the *cella*. However, as Cunliffe points out,[33] the discovery of parts of solid columns in 1897 and 1982 throws doubt on this theory. It is certain that there would have been insufficient space to provide a central *cella* surrounded by detached columns framing an ambulatory. All these styles of building are known in the Roman Empire, but at Bath it is more likely that the *cella* was plain.[34] The temple was surrounded by a paved precinct, with an altar situated in front of the temple steps, the normal layout for a classical temple, where the sacrifices were conducted outside. The enclosed sacred spring lay in the south-east corner of the temple precinct, and was directly in line with the altar to the north of it. The altar itself was free standing, raised on a platform with sculptures depicting gods and goddesses clasping its corners. There were presumably four of these, so on all four sides there would be two deities facing the viewer. Three of these sculptures have been found. The first has been lodged in the Museum for some time, but with no certain provenance. It was probably found in 1790, when the Pump Room was built, since the northern side of this eighteenth-century building cuts across the middle of the altar.[35] It depicts Hercules and Jupiter. Another stone was taken away from Bath at some unknown period in the Middle Ages, and used in the base of one of the corner buttresses of the church at Compton Dando. Having been open to the elements for about two centuries, this sculpture is badly worn, so the gods depicted on it cannot be securely identified. Fortunately the stone is now safe and well in the Museum, having been detached from the church with permission of the parish authorities and brought home. A third cornerstone turned up in the excavations of 1965, with a god identified as Bacchus on one side and an unknown goddess on the other. On each of the three extant cornerstones, one deity is shown unclothed and one clothed, so the altar perhaps showed the two clothed figures, one on each corner at front and rear, and the naked ones on the two sides. As identified the deities are all classical Roman ones, with no sculpture readily proclaiming Sulis.

The temple precincts may have been left open in this early phase, though they were eventually enclosed within a colonnade, probably in the second half of the second century. The whole complex of baths, temples and sacred spring at Bath would have been an imposing sight to the local people of the later first century AD, some three or four decades after the conquest. The younger generation that saw the temple and the baths being built would have known only a little of the way of life of the later British Iron Age, and would have had time to adjust to *Romanitas*, but the older people may have felt nostalgia for the old ways. For them, the experience of visiting the place may have been akin to going back to the shrine of Our Lady of Walsingham after being taken to see it as a child, and returning over fifty years later at the beginning of the twenty-first century. It started out as a little chapel, not much bigger than a garden shed, built near the holy well. It was small in size but loomed large in the imagination, with an air of sanctity and mystery that seemed to reach back far beyond the introduction of Christianity. Nowadays the chapel is completely subsumed in a much larger edifice, surrounded by a large and beautiful garden complex with different chapels that provide for other Christian denominations apart from Roman Catholic or Church of England, and indeed for other religions. This is exactly how the Romans organised their religious sites, where a multiplicity of gods and goddesses were represented by several different temples and shrines in various parts of their towns and cities. The visitors seeking religious solace and the tourists who go to the shrine of Our Lady of Walsingham no doubt gain tremendous satisfaction from their experience, but to the awestruck child of the 1950s, the special intimacy and simplicity of the place has been lost. It may have been the same for the older British visitors to the Roman version of the sacred springs of Bath.

1. The modern version of the King's Bath, originally built in around 1100 and named for King Henry I. This bath is situated directly above the sacred spring and the reservoir, but when the medieval builders erected this bathing establishment there was no trace of the Roman remains underneath it.

2. Artist's reconstruction in the Roman Baths Museum of the second period of the reservoir around the sacred spring, when it was completely enclosed inside a building with a vaulted roof. The King's Bath was built above this reservoir.

3. Another view of the King's Bath. On the wall to the right the statue in the ogee headed arch is the legendary King Bladud. According to the *History of the Kings of Britain*, written by Geoffrey of Monmouth around 1135, Bladud was the founder of Bath in the eighth century BC. As heir to the throne, Bladud contracted leprosy and hid himself away as a swineherd not far from Bath. He noticed that when his pigs wallowed in the hot springs, their skin sores were healed, so he tried the same cure for himself, and in gratitude when he found himself healed, he founded Bath.

Above: 4. In the nineteenth century, the arches of the King's Bath were erroneously thought to be Roman in origin, but they are not. The water is not naturally green, but derives its colour from algae, which grows well in hot water illuminated by daylight. *Below*: 5. The Great Bath, a reconstruction dating from Victorian times. The Roman bath was roofed, probably in timber in its first version, but in its second phase it was vaulted over at a much greater height than the Victorian walls would suggest. Lighting would have been provided by semi-circular windows high up in the vault, and at each end the vault would have been open to let out the steam, which is clearly visible in this photo.

Above left: 6. This classic view shows the abbey beyond the Great Bath, and demonstrates how close together they are. *Above right*: 7. Part of one of the Roman supporting arches for the vault is shown here at ground level at the end of the Great Bath. It consists of narrow tiles stacked on their ends, which would have been laid over wooden centring until the concrete was hard enough to support the arch. Just visible underneath the arch there are a series of box tiles, which were set inside the concrete of the vault to lighten the overall weight and reduce the pressure on the supporting walls. Sometimes in Roman buildings, for the same purpose of reducing weight, pottery vessels such as amphorae were placed upside down in the vault or dome, and then the concrete was poured over them, so what looks like a solid roof from the outside is in fact honeycombed inside. A notable example is the Pantheon in Rome.

Left: 8. This photo of one of the long sides of the Great Bath shows the Victorian version of the bath, with slender, round columns. Although they look authentic, these are not Roman. The concrete, vaulted roof could never have been supported on such columns. The Roman remains are the truncated stumps of massive pillars enclosing the columns, and this photo shows how the original pillars had to be massively strengthened to front and rear by extra stonework to support the vault. *Opposite*: 9. This photo shows in greater detail how the strengthening of the pillars involved carving the bases to match the originals.

10. One of the Roman rectangular pillars survives to considerable height at the corner of the Great Bath.

Left: 11. Although the modern version of the Great Bath dates from Victorian times and has no roof, this view gives some impression of the walkway around the bath itself, where the flooring consists in part of Roman paving slabs. The *exedrae* along the walls, rectangular in the centre and apsidal on either side, would have provided space for bathers to stand or sit out of splashing range. The fact that the paving around the Great Bath had to be renewed in Roman times indicates how well used the bathing facilities were.

Opposite: 12. The walkway on the south side of the Great Bath, with Roman paving stones still *in situ*. In Roman times the bathing establishment would probably have been much more ornate, the roof would have been much higher, and somewhat clumsy-looking stone pillars would probably have been painted, along with the walls, though there is no evidence for such embellishments now.

13. The modern reconstructions of corridors with vaulted roof give an idea of the appearance of the baths in Roman times, but without the decoration.

Left: 14. The modern lamp brackets on the columns may have had Roman counterparts, since there is evidence that bathing establishments were used after dark in some provinces. There is no absolute proof for late opening hours at Bath, but with such short winter days it is likely that the bathers were able to use the facilities after sunset.
Opposite: 15. This is the instantly recognisable view of the Great Bath at Bath, watched over by reproductions of Roman statues, in this case a modern Minerva complete with her helmet.

Left: 16. The modern version of the goddess Minerva above the Great Bath.

Below: 17a and b. The gilt-bronze head of Minerva found in 1727. No trace of the body of the statue has been found, but it is taken as read that this head is part of the cult statue that would have been placed inside the temple of Sulis Minerva. The goddess would have been provided with her helmet, as the casting at the rear of her head shows, but it has disappeared, probably in antiquity.

Opposite: 18. The so-called Gorgon's head from the pediment of the temple of Sulis Minerva. The goddess Minerva is usually shown in sculptures with the Gorgon's head on her breastplate, so this is how the name came to be attached to this magnificent sculpture, one of the finest from Roman Britain. Problems arise because the Gorgons were female and this sculpture is decidedly male, with flowing hair and moustaches. The face has also been interpreted as Oceanus or Neptune.

19. There was a free-standing, rectangular altar outside the temple of Sulis Minerva, facing the steps leading up to the temple entrance. This is one of a pair of sculptures that clasped one of the corners of the altar. All four corners were probably decorated in the same way but only three such double-figures have been found; two at Bath and one at the parish church at Compton Dando, now removed and placed inside the Roman Baths Museum. This figure is interpreted as Hercules Bibax, with his lion skin hung around his shoulders, secured by knotting the forepaws across the chest of the god. Hercules is accompanied by Jupiter, not shown here, identified by his sceptre and staff, and his eagle on his left. All the gods and goddesses on the three double-sculptures at the corners of the altar are classical Roman deities.

20. The temple would always have been served by a priest and his staff, but the only evidence for a priest derives from this tombstone, appropriately shaped for him like an altar. It was found around 1795 at Bathwick. The tombstone was set up by Calpurnia Trifosa for her husband Gaius Calpurnius Receptus, who died aged seventy-five. He is described as *sacerdos deae Sulis*, priest of the goddess Sulis, which fortunately removes any doubt about his relationship to the temple.

Opposite: 21. The sculptured head interpreted as Luna, goddess of the moon, found in 1790 when the Pump Room was being rebuilt. This head or bust may have been placed in the pediment of a façade or a building opposite the sacred spring on the north side of the temple precinct. Together with other fragmentary sculptures, this structure is labelled by modern archaeologists as the façade of the Four Seasons. It may have been simply a wall bearing relief sculptures, or it may have been the front of a building, possibly another temple.

22. The hot springs still faithfully deliver hot water for the baths, staining everything orange from the iron content of the water. The arch shown here is Roman work, but this is not thought to be the original inlet for the spring water in Roman times.

23. Though the hot water from the spring arrives effortlessly into the baths, the flow has to be managed, and the water for the conventional baths with warm rooms, hot rooms and plunge baths, has to be conducted into the various pools. This lead pipe, still *in situ* in its groove in the paving, is one small part of the elaborate Roman plumbing system. There was no shortage of lead in Bath, since there were mines at Charterhouse in the Mendips, not too far away from the town. The Romans were mining the lead there within six years of the Claudian conquest in AD 43.

Right & Below right: 24a. and b.
The management of the water supply
involved letting the water in and also
allowing it to flow out. The Romans
were experienced and accomplished
water engineers, and at Bath they
understood that culverts and drains
had to be large enough to allow access
to clean and flush them, because the
build-up of mud from the hot springs
would eventually clog up the system.
Manholes were placed above the
drains at points where it was expected
that blockages might occur. The
wastewater was led out from the baths
to the River Avon.

25. Reconstruction in the Roman Baths Museum of the bathing establishment, showing the vault over the Great Bath and the transverse vault over the so-called Lucas Bath. The three shorter vaults are those of the eastern range of conventional baths. To the right is the round temple, called the *tholos*, thought to have been located underneath the western end of the abbey.

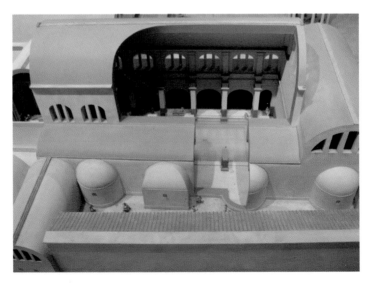

26. This cut-away reconstruction shows the interior of the Roman bath, and the semi-circular windows high up in the sides of the vault. Along the side can be seen the roofs of the three *exedrae*, the central one rectangular, flanked by two apsidal ones.

27. The relationship of the baths to the temple and its enclosed precinct is shown in this model in the Roman Baths Museum. This is the later phase of the temple and baths, when the sacred spring had been enclosed within a vaulted building, visible here at the top right of the photo.

Right: 28. The *tepidarium* and the *caldarium* of the conventional baths at the eastern and western ends of the Great Bath required heating from furnaces, conducted under the floors through the hypocaust system. These stacked tiles formed the supports for one of the floors in the western baths, which would probably have been embellished by mosaics. The floors could have attained considerable heat and people visiting the baths would have needed their sandals. *Above*: 29. Box tiles could be used in vaulted roofs to lessen the weight of the concrete, but they could also be used to conduct heat from the hypocausts along the walls of a building.

30. The Roman town of Aquae Sulis was only very small compared to other Romano-British towns and its status within the framework of local government is unknown. This reconstruction in the Roman Baths Museum shows how the baths and the temple of Sulis Minerva filled the greater part of the settlement. The conjectural theatre is shown to the north of the baths, though there is no evidence that this is where it stood. The plan of the main streets and the gates is less conjectural, but the buildings all around the temple and baths are mostly guesswork, based on the excavations that have taken place in small areas of the modern town.

31. This is the top part of tombstone of a cavalryman, though it is not known who he was, because the accompanying inscription has been lost. Although the stone is carved in the same conventional form, showing the rider moving to the right, it does not fit well with the lower section of Tancinus's tombstone, so it belongs to a different soldier.

32. A sculpture usually interpreted as a theatrical mask, showing a face with half-open mouth. It is not certain where it was found, but since it is thought to have been a funerary monument and since Roman law forbade burials inside the town, it would probably have been placed somewhere along one of the roads leading out of the town.

Right: 34. This individual has lost his head and his feet, and has no explanatory inscription to tell us who he was. The stone was probably found near the North Gate, which would indicate that it is a tombstone. The detailed depiction of the folds of his clothing show how his tunic and cloak were arranged. He wears a belt and carries a sword in a scabbard on his left side, so he was probably a soldier.

Opposite page: 33. The people of Aquae Sulis are attested by the sculptures, inscriptions and artefacts they left behind them. This is a typical cavalry tombstone, the top portion of which has been lost. It shows the trooper Lucius Vitellius Tancinus riding down a hapless barbarian under the horse's hooves. This was conventional portraiture, with the cavalryman usually riding to the right, so as to show his spear in his right hand.

35. Found in two sections which join up, this is another tombstone found near the North Gate. The man is framed in a niche and enveloped in his cloak, fastened by a brooch. His hands are clasped in front of him, holding an object which defies interpretation. His hairstyle and his beard lend support to the theory that he lived in the reign of Hadrian, when beards became fashionable.

36a and b. These two views of a lady's head with elaborate hairstyle belong to a very early context of Roman Bath. Such massed curls are typical of the Flavian period, as demonstrated by portraits of Domitia, wife of the Emperor Domitian, who was assassinated in AD 96. Even if fashions in Roman Britain lagged behind those of Rome, this lady would have been one of the earliest visitors or settlers in Aquae Sulis, which was founded around AD 75. Unfortunately it is not known who she was.

Above: 37. Mask of beaten tin, found in the main culvert of the Roman baths. It is similar to masks found in France in the context of religious establishments. It may have been worn by a priest at religious ceremonies, or perhaps more likely attached to a wooden support and carried, possibly as a representation of a native god.

Right: 38a, b, c, d. Offerings made to Sulis and thrown into the sacred spring include items of pewter or more rarely silver, such as flagons and *paterae*, or saucepans with handles, sometimes inscribed with the words 'Deae Suli' or 'Sulis', to the goddess Sulis. The items may have been dedicated in anticipation of the answer to a prayer, or in thanks for a prayer that had been granted.

Left: 39. Detail of a sculpture which shows a large dog carrying a roe-deer across its back. This photo shows the head of the deer grasped in the dog's mouth. The teeth can be seen round the deer's neck. It was found near Bath at Walcot, and may have been part of a funerary monument.

Below & bottom: 40a. and b. These figures are part of a mosaic floor that was found in the north-east part of Aquae Sulis when alterations were made to the Bluecoat School in 1859. The animals are sea creatures whose bodies end in curled tails, and dolphins swim near to them.

Opposite: 41. Tombstone of Julius Vitalis, armourer of Legio XX Valeria Victrix. He was not yet thirty years old when he died at Bath, and his colleagues paid for this stone to be put up. (*RIB* I 156)

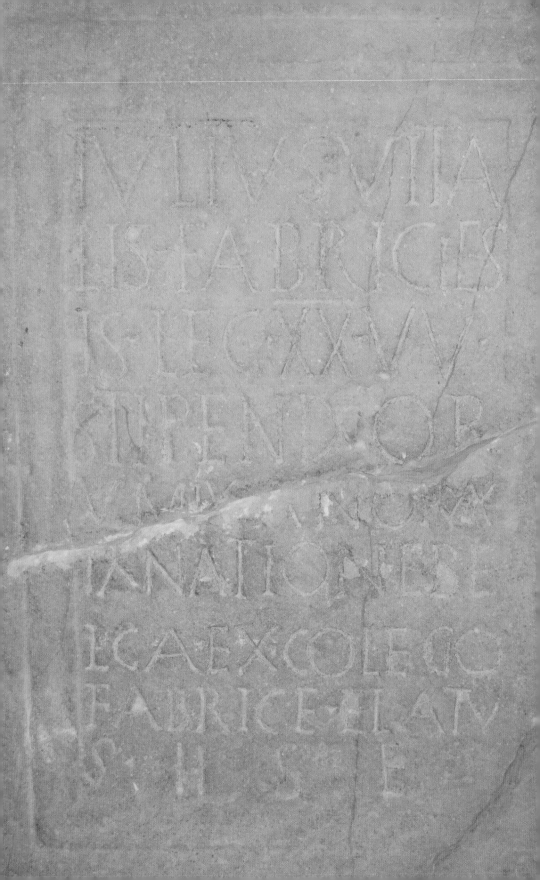

```
MIVSMIA[
...IS·FABRICES
IS·LEG·XX·V·V
N·PEND·OR
...ANORVM
IANATIONESE
LCA·EX·COLEGO
FABRICE·LLATV
S·H·S·E
```

Above: 42. Inscription from a tombstone recording Antigonus, a soldier of Legio XX who died at Bath aged forty-five. Since the legion does not bear its title Valeria Victrix, awarded after the rebellion of Boudicca, it is possible, but by no means proven, that the tomb dates from the period before AD 60–1. (*RIB* I 160)

Left: 43. This altar, broken into two sections, records a vow made to the goddess Sulis by the freedman Aufidius Eutuches for the welfare and safety of his former master, centurion of Legio VI Victrix, who was stationed at York. (*RIB* I 143)

44. This is another altar dedicated to the goddess Sulis for the health and safety of the centurion Marcus Aufidius Maximus, this time by his freedman Aufidius Lemnus. (*RIB* I 144)

45. The first line of this inscription starts with the letters '... NA', which does not make sense unless there had been a line above it, now erased, showing the first part of the name of the goddess Diana. It is an altar dedicated by the freedman Vettius Benignus. (*RIB* I 138)

46. This altar has had its top broken off. It was dedicated to the god Loucetius Mars and the goddess Nemetona by Peregrinus, a citizen of Trier. (*RIB* I 140)

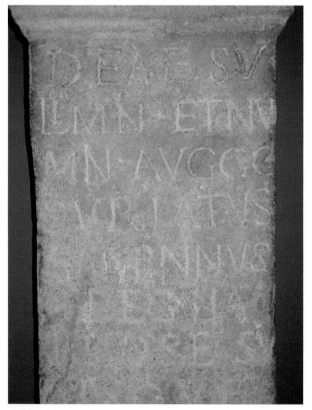

47. Gaius Curiatius Saturninus, centurion of Legio II Augusta, dedicated this altar to the goddess Sulis and the divine spirit of the two Emperors, probably Marcus Aurelius and his colleague Lucius Verus. (*RIB* I 146)

Above: 48. This stone is broken so the name of the man who set it up is not known, except that he was the son of Novantius. He set up the inscription as the result of a vision. (*RIB* I 153)

Right: 49. Sulinus the sculptor, son of Brucetus, set up this base for a statue, dedicated to the three mother goddesses, the Suleviae. Sulinus, son of Brucetus, is also known from Cirencester where he may have had a workshop. The statue that adorned this stone, presumably made by Sulinus himself, is not known. (*RIB* I 151)

50. The mother goddesses always came in threes, so this crudely executed sculpture of three females may represent them. There may be a connection with the Suleviae, worshipped by Sulinus, son of Brucetus, though there is no evidence for this suggestion. The stone was found at Bathwick, with the right-hand edge missing, so it is not known if all three figures wore the same pleated skirts.

51. Priscus, son of Toutis, declares himself a stonemason (*lapidarius*) in this dedication to the goddess Sulis. Priscus was a citizen of the Carnutes tribe, whose capital was at Chartres. It is possible but not proven that he may have worked on one or more of the buildings at Aquae Sulis. (*RIB* I 149)

52. This stone records some sacrilegious damage done to a monument or a building, repaired by Gaius Severius Emeritus, centurion in charge of the region. His title is expressed as a reversed 'C', standing for centurion, and the abbreviation 'REG', inserted at the bottom as though it was an afterthought. (*RIB* I 152)

53. One of the first curse tablets found in the reservoir underneath the King's Bath when it was excavated in 1880. This is the famous Vilbia, stolen away by persons unknown, though suspects Velvinna, Exsuperus, Severinus, Augustalis, Comitianus, Catusminianus, Germanilla and Jovina, are named. Though the curse was obviously placed in the sacred spring for the attention of the goddess Sulis, she is not actually mentioned in the text. Presumably she would have known who the victim was, and who or what Vilbia was, which is more than modern interpreters can guess. (*RIB* I 154)

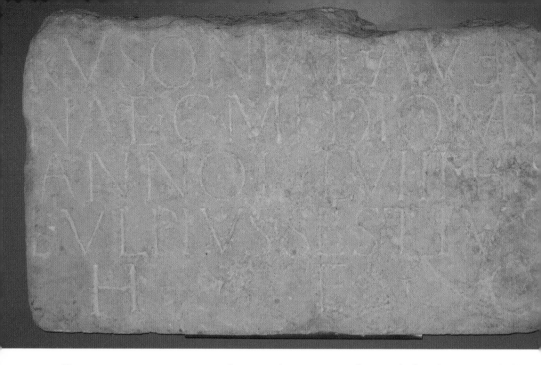

54. Not many women are represented among the inscriptions from Bath, but there are probably several tombstones on the roads leading out of the town that have not yet been found. This is the grave of Rusonia Aventina, a citizen of the Mediomatrici, whose tribal centre was at Metz. She was fifty-eight years old when she died. (*RIB* I 163)

55. This tombstone was set up for a child, Mercatilla, whose short life ended after only one year, six months and twelve days. She was the foster daughter of Magnius. (*RIB* I 162)

4

BATH FLOURISHES

It is a measure of the success of the religious healing centre and the bathing establishments at Aquae Sulis that within about fifty years after the foundation of the baths and the temple, improvements and extensions began, the first of a continuing series of alterations in which the temple of Sulis Minerva was enlarged and the baths at the east and west ends of the Great Bath were made more and more elaborate.

Most of the archaeological attention has been focused on the temple, the enclosed sacred spring, and the Great Bath with its attendant conventional baths, but the Romans did not limit their development of the town to the most powerful spring. Investigation of the south-west area of Bath, just behind the temple of Sulis Minerva, has been less intense, but it was discovered in excavations of 1987 that the spring serving what later became the Cross Bath was enclosed inside an oval wall. The date when this was done is not known, and there may have been no facilities for bathing here. It is suggested that the pool was left open, as a sacred place for private veneration. On two occasions in the nineteenth century the cistern of the Cross Bath required cleaning: in 1809, when an altar to Sulis Minerva was found[1] and in 1885. During the second cleaning process a sculptured block was dug out, with scenes carved on it representing Aesculapius, the important Roman god of healing, whose temple on the Tiber Island in Rome is now a church dedicated to St Bartholomew, with a continued tradition of healing.

The Hot Bath was also patronised by the Romano-Britons of Aquae Sulis, as revealed by the discovery of three altars. In the later eighteenth century, when the spring was being cleared out, the workers found a dedication to Sulis Minerva[2] possibly dating to the second century AD. Two years later in 1776 another altar turned up, dedicated to the goddess Diana.[3] The third inscription, dug out in 1825, is the lower half of a building block, so the full text has not survived. It was set up by someone whose full name is missing, except that he was the son of Novantius.[4] Intriguingly, he set up the inscription for himself and his family as the result of a vision that he had experienced (*ex visu*). He may have been the founder of a religious building or a bathing establishment, and although no linkage with the unknown son of Novantius can be proven, there was a suite of baths at the Hot Bath spring. Part of this building was discovered and recorded when the foundations for the Royal United Hospital were being laid in 1864–66. The Novantius stone came from the area south-west of Stall Street at Lower Borough Walls. These Hot Spring baths were too elaborate for a private house so it is assumed that the suite was a public building. It was preceded by an earlier building, the remains of which were found underneath it, but not certainly identified.[5]

The depiction of Aesculapius shows that the curative powers of the waters were recognised even if not actually used at the Cross Bath, and the dedications to Sulis at the Cross Bath and the Hot Bath confirm that she was the presiding deity of all three springs.

Much more is known about the alterations to the temple of Sulis Minerva, the sacred spring and the main bathing establishment. In the second century AD the wall surrounding the sacred spring was heightened and the pool was completely enclosed within a rectangular building; the temple of Sulis Minerva was enlarged; the western end of the baths was rebuilt on a larger scale and with a more sophisticated plan; and the so-called 1923 bath at the eastern end was filled in and a new suite of conventional baths was installed. The late-first-century building had been splendid enough, but by the beginning of the third century the religious precinct and the bath complex was infinitely more elaborate. The place would still have been recognisable to a first-century visitor transported to the future, but it would probably have seemed somewhat bewildering, something akin to someone doing the shopping in a 1950s high street suddenly transported to a modern mall with all the glitter and hype.

It is not possible to ascertain precise dates for the successive modifications that were carried out at different periods in the history of the Roman baths and temple. Archaeological excavations have revealed distinct phases in each of the areas that have been investigated, but it is difficult to establish whether the identifiable phases in one part of the bathing establishment are contemporary with those of another section, so a definitive chronology cannot be achieved. The alterations that were made in the baths, the sacred pool and the temple in the second century may have been carried out as part of a centralised plan, and put into effect continuously over a period of several years, or they may have been the result of successive plans for remodelling different parts of the whole temple and baths complex as and when opportunity arose. This uncertainty renders the task of sorting out the cumulative picture more problematic. Given the difficult circumstances of excavating the Roman buildings, obscured as they are by medieval and modern structures, it is truly remarkable that so much has been discovered, enabling archaeologists to use informed speculation to interpret the various remains.

The first alterations to the religious and bathing complex may belong to the reign of Hadrian, who was Emperor from AD 117 to 138. From the latter years of the reign of Domitian, assassinated in AD 96, through to the accession of Hadrian, the main focus of the Roman Imperial government was on the Danube, and then briefly on the eastern provinces. In the late AD 80s the tribes of Dacia (modern Romania) poured over the Danube and successively destroyed two Roman armies. The Emperor Domitian was raising a third army when he was assassinated in AD 96. His successor Nerva died in AD 98, so it was left to the next Emperor, Trajan, to wage two major wars to solve the Dacian problem. During this period, the province of Britain was not of the foremost importance to the Emperors. The need for troops to combat the Dacians overrode any consideration of further expansion and military consolidation in Britain. There was a comprehensive withdrawal from Scotland, which had only very recently been conquered by Gnaeus Julius Agricola. The furthest northern boundary in the reign of Trajan was redrawn in the Tyne–Solway gap across what is now Northumberland and Cumbria.

In the southern parts of Britain, while there was not complete stagnation in the towns at the opening years of the second century, in the reign of Hadrian there was a detectable advancement and growth in Romano-British towns in the form of new or enlarged public buildings and the improvement of civic amenities. Hadrian was the first Emperor to turn away from the concept of *imperium sine fine*, power without end, the entrenched attitude which contributed to the hitherto unquestioned certainty that the destiny of Rome was to go ever onwards, making conquests and adding territory to the Empire. Hadrian called a halt, turning territorial boundaries that were not necessarily fixed into more permanent frontiers, some of them delineated by a physical barrier, some of them marked by lines of watchtowers and forts. Hadrian visited most of the provinces of the Roman Empire and came to Britain in AD 122. He probably rode along the Tyne–Solway gap, where the central sector ran along the north-facing cliff of the Whin Sill, a divine geological gift to an Emperor who wanted to create a north-facing frontier line.

Hadrian probably also investigated for himself what was happening in the towns, and perhaps made some suggestions. There are no absolutely precise dates for redevelopment in various towns, but in general it seems that the surge of detectable building work was Hadrianic.[6] At Silchester the timber forum, one of the very earliest in the country, was replaced by a stone version[7] and at Cirencester the basilica was reconstructed.[8] The forum and the public baths at Wroxeter, which may have had a first phase that was allowed to lapse unfinished, were completed, as well as a marketplace, or *macellum*.[9] Near the main entrance on the eastern side of the forum at Wroxeter, several pieces of a massive inscription[10] were found in 1924, naming the Emperor Hadrian with all his titles. It was set up in his honour by the *civitas Cornoviorum*, in the fourteenth year of the Emperor's tribunician power, which dates the inscription to December AD 129 to December AD 130. This probably commemorates the dedication of the completed forum. Something similar may have happened to the public administrative buildings at Caerwent at around the same time, and there is a hint that the first defences around the town were built around AD 130.

There are inferences that Hadrian instigated some administrative reforms in Roman Britain by dividing the larger *civitates* into smaller units. The extensive *civitas Brigantum*, based on Aldborough in Yorkshire, contained several smaller tribes, and at some point these were given their own capitals. Carlisle became the *civitas* capital of the Carvetii, the Parisi were based on Brough on Humber, and the civil settlement at Corbridge became the *civitas* of the Corionototae.[11] In the south, Ilchester was made an independent *civitas*, divorced from local government by the *civitas* of the Durotriges at Dorchester, and the tribe of the Demetae, hitherto joined with the Dobunni, were given a capital next to the *vicus* outside the fort at Carmarthen. In the poorer area of the Fens, an attempt was made to drain the land and encourage farming and salt making, and it seems that there was an increase in the size of the population in Hadrian's reign. There were efforts to boost the *civitas* capital of the Iceni at Caistor by Norwich, which had never really flourished since its foundation. The standard of living seemed to improve in many areas of Britain, at least for the wealthy. Bigger and better town houses stared to appear, and in the countryside more villas were built and the older ones were improved.

Continuing Alterations to the Bathing Complex at Aquae Sulis

It is in this context of reinvigorated building in the towns during the reign of Emperor Hadrian that the first alterations at Bath probably began. Hadrian may have visited the place, and given that he always displayed an interest in the details of how things were run, he may even have provided part of the necessary finance, though there is no evidence to support this.

The alterations were quite extensive. Both ends of the bathing complex underwent rebuilding operations, to improve the facilities at the western baths and to create a new suite of conventional baths at the eastern end. There is only slight evidence, apart from the background of the general but widespread second-century context of refurbishment and new building, to suggest that the improvements at the Roman baths were Hadrianic in date. Pottery fragments dated to the period around AD 100 to AD 125 were found in the excavation of the second phase of the conventional baths at the western end of the bathing complex. This provides properly attested archaeological evidence for the commencement of the building work in the second quarter of the second century, after AD 125 but probably before AD 138, when Hadrian died.

There is another inference, rather than hard evidence, that points to a Hadrianic context for the first major alteration of the baths. In some of the more important towns in the Roman Empire, bathing establishments often possessed two sets of baths. Most likely one was for men and one for women, notably at the Stabian Baths at Pompeii, but there was not usually any proper partition between the two suites, and sometimes the swimming pools were shared by both sexes. In the early Empire, mixed bathing was at first frowned upon, but was gradually accepted, until increasingly scandalous behaviour in the baths threw the practice into ill repute. The Emperor Hadrian passed a law to put an end to mixed bathing and bring some decorum to the proceedings. The source for this derives from the biography of Hadrian in the collected works previously known as the *Scriptores Historiae Augustae*, now abbreviated to *Historia Augusta*. This work picks up where Suetonius Tranquillus left off in the *Twelve Caesars*, but does not share the same reputation for reliability. It purports to be a collection of biographies by different writers but it has been established that there was only one author, who tended to dwell on the scandalous and shocking rather than the historically useful facts. However, it is sometimes the only source and with caution it is accepted that Hadrian made some alteration to the use of public baths, at some unknown date between his accession in AD 117 and his death in AD 138. He separated men and women in the baths[12] and decreed that only invalids, and probably women, could use the baths in the mornings.[13] The law forbidding mixed bathing was perhaps not fully effective, since similar legislation was reissued by the Emperor Marcus Aurelius towards the end of the second century, and by Severus Alexander in the early third century.[14]

It may have been in response to the Hadrianic legislation that in the second century, possibly after Hadrian himself had visited Britain in AD 122, the Roman baths at Aquae Sulis were converted to provide two separate bathing suites.[15] In order to comply with the law, there were two choices for bathing facilities. At the smaller bathing establishments, where there was no room for expansion, or perhaps no money to pay for alterations, the operators usually allocated one set of opening hours for women, who probably bathed in the mornings, and another for men, who used the baths in the afternoons.[16] This practice necessarily restricted the numbers of people that could be admitted at any one time, so the provision of two sets of baths would ensure that more people could be catered for during the day, and the male and female visitors to the baths were not inconvenienced by adherence to strictly divided opening hours. After the Hadrianic law was passed, whoever was in charge at Aquae Sulis probably considered that timely alterations to the eastern end of the baths would serve better than restrictions on opening hours.

At the eastern end of the baths the conversion involved changing the rectangular bath, the so-called 1923 bath, into a conventional bathing establishment with *tepidarium* and *caldarium*. The 1923 bath had been supplied with water by a pipe from the Lucas Bath, so the first task was to divert the water into the outlet drain. Traces of the stone channel made for this purpose are still visible. The next task was to fill in the now redundant rectangular bath and start building afresh to provide a strongly constructed flue on the north side and a heating system that would supply under-floor heating for the *tepidarium* and *caldarium*, and also hot water to make the steam for the latter room. The walls of the new building were much thicker than the first version, possibly to accommodate the pressure of a vaulted roof.

The rooms of the eastern baths were fewer and smaller than the western baths, and in view of the dearth of any hard evidence it is probably rash, but tempting, to view these smaller rooms as the facilities offered for exclusive use by women. The excavators themselves suggested that the second set of conventional baths on the eastern end of the complex may have been built in order to provide separate facilities so that men and women could use the baths simultaneously. Until further evidence comes to light to prove or disprove this theory, it is a good working hypothesis that in the reign of Hadrian,[17] either in response to the new legislation or simply in response to increased demand, the decision was taken to rebuild the two ends of the baths. This indicates that enough people were using the baths by the early second century to warrant the expenditure of time and money to improve and enlarge the establishment.

The alterations to the western baths created facilities that were somewhat more elaborate than the small set of baths at the eastern end.[18] In the first phase, these conventional western baths had projected south of the outer wall of the Great Bath. The eastern wall of this projection had been aligned to the wall dividing the entrance hall or *frigidarium*, from the Great Bath. In the second phase, the southern end of the conventional baths was extended further eastwards, so as to wrap right around the external south-west corner of the Great Bath. The conventional bathing establishment was converted into a much larger and more sophisticated system than its predecessor.

There were two entrances/exits to the extended version of the baths. One entrance led along the southern exterior wall of the Great Bath into an entrance hall, with a small bath on the left-hand side of it. Seen in isolation, the position of this entrance is somewhat strangely located, but the excavators conjectured that to the south of the Great Bath, there may have been an exercise area,[19] so people using this doorway into the baths would have been already inside the complex and not approaching from the streets to come right up against the wall of the Great Bath. An exercise area would have been a normal adjunct to a bathing establishment in any part of the Roman world. Most of the important baths in the Roman Empire had facilities for other leisure activities as well as exercising. At Aquae Sulis, when the first alterations were made, there may have been an enclosed space for athletics, either in the open air, or possibly there was even a roofed building, with maybe space for a library and intellectual pursuits. Unfortunately, modern buildings obscure this area south of the Great Bath and the conventional baths, and until there is opportunity to excavate, all this speculation must remain an unconfirmed but likely theory.

Approaching the baths from the oddly sited doorway against the south wall of the Great Bath, visitors would turn right to go through a doorway giving access to a corridor, which ran right through the newly built western baths, leading in one direction to the other entrance/exit in the western wall, and in the opposite direction the corridor lined up exactly with the walkway all along the south side of the Great Bath and the Lucas Bath. Visitors seeking curative facilities could turn right to enter the Great Bath, or those wishing only to cleanse themselves could turn left to enter the improved conventional bathing complex at the western end of the building.

On the right of the visitor coming westwards along the corridor there was the old entrance hall or *frigidarium*, now altered beyond recognition with a circular pool inside it, appropriately labelled by archaeologists the Circular Bath, the remains of which are on view for modern visitors to the Museum. This was a cold-water plunge bath, supplied via a fountain in its north wall. Excess water ran off into an overflow heading ultimately towards the south-east corner of the baths, and from there into the sewers and eventually the drainage culvert running along the south side of the whole bathing establishment.[20] From the paved surface of the former hall or *frigidarium*, visitors 'taking the plunge' would descend the stone steps of the Circular Bath, which was about 1.5 metres deep. It was most probably once lined with paving slabs covered with a layer of lead, but unfortunately the floor has disappeared, leaving only rubble for the excavators to find at the bottom of the pool, so there is now no evidence for this reasonable assumption that it was stone-flagged and lead-lined.

Other doors on the west and east sides of the room containing the Circular Bath gave access respectively to the *tepidarium* of the western baths and the Great Bath. In the *frigidarium* of the first phase of the baths, there had been free access at the north end of the room, where visitors could view the sacred spring, but when the Circular Bath was installed this view was blocked off by a wall that ran from side to side of the former hall, linking the two pillars that supported the roof at the northern end. The height of this internal wall is not known; it may or may not have extended as far as the roof. Beyond this wall, the remaining northern part of the former hall was converted into a small corridor, entered only from the Great Bath. Since the short corridor did not lead anywhere else, the suggestion that it was a viewing platform for the spring is the most feasible. Also the wall closing off the Circular Bath served to prevent visitors who simply wanted to see the hot springs from gazing at the bathers on the other side. The two original pillars supporting the roof were left visible as part of the new dividing wall, and on the surfaces that faced into the viewing corridor, the fluted decoration did not reach the original floor level, so the excavators suggested that the corridor floor had been raised to enable visitors to view the spring. This was made necessary by the fact that the wall around the spring had been built up by about 1 metre, so unless the viewers were standing on a raised floor they would not have been able to see into the pool.

Passage into the *tepidarium* of the new, improved western baths was only possible from the Circular Bath, and from the *tepidarium* visitors could enter the *caldarium*. There was no direct access to the warm and hot rooms from the corridor, which would have taken the visitor heading westwards to two rooms on the left-hand, or south, side. The first has been labelled the *apodyterium*, where visitors prepared themselves for the baths and left their clothes, and the other was an entirely new feature. The visitor would turn left into a recess, then straight on through a doorway into a vestibule, and then right into a small circular room known as a *laconicum*, where the heating system provided intense dry heat to induce sweating, in the same way as a modern sauna.

The new, improved baths at the western end of the complex now provided for a variety of different experiences. After enjoying the Roman version of a sauna the visitor could simply go home, or continue his or her progress through the *tepidarium* and *caldarium*, and then plunge into the Circular Bath or the Great Bath, combining all or some of the features of the baths as he or she wished. It was now a much more sophisticated establishment than it was in its first phase.

The alterations to the western and eastern ends of the baths may have been started at different times, but it is more likely that they took place simultaneously according to one overall plan. There is not enough precise dating evidence for the building work to ascertain exactly when it was carried out, or how long it took to complete the project. Presumably some part of the baths, or possibly the whole complex, would have to be closed while materials were brought in and building work was going on, so the duration of the proceedings could have been quite prolonged. The same problems of dating apply to all the successive phases of the baths. At least four more building phases have been identified, of which the third and fourth are briefly described here, and the final two late Roman phases will be outlined in the next chapter.

The most monumental of these successive alterations to the bath complex was the complete re-roofing that was carried out, perhaps in the later second century.[21] This massive project entailed dismantling the first roofing system, which is generally considered to have been of timber with a tiled pitched roof covering the exterior. The wood had most likely suffered in the steamy atmosphere of the Great Bath. Once demolition had finished, the new concrete vault could be started. This is the more usual type of roof for Roman bath houses because it is more resistant to steam, but though the main advantage of a concrete vault is that it is less prone to rot, its main disadvantage is that it is enormously heavy compared to timber posts and tiles. The Romans had found a way of reducing the weight in concrete vaults and domes by including pottery vessels in the structure, such as amphorae, placed upside down so the concrete could be poured over them, leaving weightless hollow spaces. The rigidity and strength of the roof was not impaired but the weight was considerably lessened. A series of box tiles built into the vault of the Great Bath appear to have served the same purpose of reducing the overall weight of the roof. Even so, the stone pillars that had supported the first roof, however it was made, had to be strengthened to take the enormous thrust of the new vault. If the existing metre-high remains of the Roman stone pillars are viewed from their sides, the measures taken to strengthen them can be clearly seen. At the front and rear of each pier there is additional stonework, with straight joints between the original and the strengthening stone. The operation was not as straightforward as it might seem since the carved projecting bases of the original piers would have to be chiselled off and the two sets of new stones carved to fit together properly and match the design. The strengthening measure indicates that the builders knew all about the weight and thrust of the new vaulted roof and had planned for it.

The main vault ran west to east over the Great Bath, and would have been open at both ends to let the steam out via a semi-circular lunette. Still visible at one end of the Great Bath is an arch that formed one of the lunettes. It is formed from tiles placed vertically on their ends, with some stacked tiles laid flat on top, and gives some idea of the size and shape of the support for the open-ended vault. Initially the vaulted roof would have been laid on wooden centring, left in place until the concrete had dried. It is to be presumed that while the roofing work was going on, the public were not allowed into the Great Bath, which may have been drained by directing the water from the spring directly into the outlet and incidentally flushing out the sand and mud in the process. If the spring waters had still been allowed to run through the Great Bath there would have been lots of steam, which might have interfered with the setting process of the concrete, but since the Romans discovered how to make concrete that would set underwater, this may not have been a problem.

It is not certain what the roof of the Lucas Bath would have been like. It may have been a vault built at right angles to the roof of the Great Bath, running north to south, and set lower so that the lunette at the eastern end of the main roof would not be obscured, and the steam could vent properly. The refurbished eastern baths may also have been vaulted, parallel to the Lucas Bath.

There was probably a row of clerestory windows on the long sides of the main vault, set high up to let light in. The ambulatories on the north and south sides of the Great Bath were vaulted separately, like the side aisles of a basilica-type church, with their roofs lower than the main roof so as not to obscure the windows. These lower vaults would also absorb some of the thrust of the new main vault, rather like a continuous buttress, but just to make sure, the Roman builders strengthened the external walls as well as the piers along the sides of the Great Bath. The two semi-circular *exedrae* or apses, and the central rectangular one on each of the long walls, were already outlined by piers on either side, acting like a frame, but these were apparently not considered strong enough, so new and larger stone piers were added to these, and the rectangular *exedrae* also received strengthening piers at their internal angles.

The layout of the Great Bath as it stands nowadays is impressive enough, but it does not reproduce the appearance of the Roman version, nor does it represent a conventional Roman bathing establishment where people went to get clean. With the aid of reconstruction paintings, a vivid imagination, a gloomier interior full of steam, and walls supporting the vault at twice the height of the present walls, with a soundtrack of splashing water and conversation, shrieks, yells, and maybe strings of oaths in Latin and Celtic languages, it might be possible to experience what it would have been like underneath the new vaulted roof of the Roman spa bath.

Probably as part of this massive refurbishment, the eastern and western baths were altered and enlarged yet again. Both the east and west baths probably each received a new vaulted roof at the same time as the work on the main vault was being carried out. The eastern baths were extended to the south of their original outline and more heated rooms were built. The western baths were also extended at the west end, where small, heated rooms were added, closing off the earlier west–east corridor. A new entrance was created where there had been a room off the corridor leading into the *laconicum* or hot dry room. Visitors now came in at this point with the *apodyterium* on the right-hand side and the *laconicum* on the left. This may have been done to ensure a better regulated flow of traffic through the building, based on people's preferences. The two sets of conventional baths may have been even larger than their appearance on plan, because as always the area of the excavations at Bath is necessarily limited to the available space or temporary access underneath modern buildings. Roman Bath in the late second century was probably one of the most spectacular establishments in Britain.

The rebuilding work presumably had one main purpose; to accommodate a greater number of visitors by offering them a greater number of facilities. Most of these would be related to visitors seeking cures or remedies for different ailments, or at least some relief from suffering.

The Development of the Sacred Spring and the Temple Precinct

The religious functions of the spa town were just as vital to the curative process as the use of the hot springs. Although several other gods and goddesses were worshipped at Bath besides Sulis Minerva, the great temple nearest to the hot spring and sacred pool would provide the chief focus for the religious needs of the visitors hoping for cures. In the second century AD the temple was enlarged by the creation of a walkway or ambulatory,[22] for which purpose the plinth of the temple was extended on three sides, while the eastern entrance and the steps leading up to it were left as they were and still open to view, except that the flight of steps was renewed. The appearance of the superstructure of the ambulatory is not certain. It could have been left as an open, roofless platform, but since it was wide enough to support columns defining the outer edge of the walkway there may have been a colonnade with a sloping roof surrounding the temple on the north, west and south sides. Alternatively, but perhaps less likely, all three sides may have been enclosed within walls. In either case, the roof would have been at a lower level than the roof of the temple, and the addition of the ambulatory all around the temple would have converted the classical building into a so-called Romano-Celtic temple.

At some time in the later second century AD the entire temple precinct was enclosed within a colonnade. The enlargement of the temple and this surrounding colonnade may have been part of a single rebuilding scheme, but the work cannot be dated. All that can be said is that at the beginning of the third century the temple area was entered from the east side through a gateway in the wall, leading into a rectangular precinct with the temple and altar in the middle and the Great Bath on the left. It seems certain that a colonnade ran round the north, west and south sides of this large enclosure. Excavations in the 1960s revealed flat stone blocks that would have provided foundations for columns set 3 metres distant from the outer walls, and in front of the foundations there was a gutter, which indicates that the colonnaded walkway probably had a tiled roof sloping inwards, with provision for the run-off of rainwater, a necessary precaution in all the provinces of the Roman Empire but perhaps even more necessary in Britain.

When the new flight of steps leading up to the temple was excavated, the older steps were revealed underneath them.[23] It was discovered that the limestone slabs of the second phase had undergone repair at least once. The steps had been cut back to allow for the insertion of new treads. The wearing down of the steps indicates a large volume of human traffic entering and exiting the temple, a high volume of footfall as it is termed nowadays.

On either side of the steps, two small shrines were erected. The southern one could not be investigated because it is covered by the Pump Room, but there were some remains of the northern one that showed that its door was in the centre of the eastern face. It would have been more pleasing to the eye if these shrines were the same size and plan and symmetrically placed on either side of the steps, so reconstruction drawings usually depict them in this way.[24] No information was recovered to suggest which deities were worshipped in these shrines.

Probably at the same time as the alterations to the temple were carried out, the hot spring was also re-developed. The surrounding wall was built up about 1 metre higher, and the whole pool was enclosed within a rectangular building with a vaulted concrete roof. A doorway was made in the north wall of the new building, so that entrance could be gained from the temple precincts, but since the floor level inside the pool was at the same height as the new wall around it, three steps were inserted to bring the doorstep in line with the interior. Inside the pool, stone bases were discovered, arranged around the edge, some square, some round. These may have supported statues of different gods, and probably columns. Reconstruction drawings of the enclosed pool usually include the statues swathed in steam from the hot spring, and plants and ferns growing inside the building. The effect was probably like a grotto or a cave where potent deities dwelt. Such mystical features have not yet been entirely eradicated from the human psyche.

When the surrounding wall of the pool was built up to its new height, the sluice that served to drain the pool from time to time was now at a lower level. Access to it was via steps down to the level of the sluice so that it could be opened when necessary, though at one time it was suggested that this arrangement was made to allow people to drink the waters. The semi-circular arch through which the orange waters cascade nowadays is not thought to be the original Roman outlet, but a relieving arch to support the new wall.

Evidence for the vaulted roof was found inside the pool where it had fallen down. Enough remnants survived for archaeologists to be able to reconstruct it. Brick arches were erected along the long sides of the rectangular building, and the weight of the concrete vault was relieved by the insertion of box tiles. Even so, there were problems with the vault later on. At the south side, the wall of the *frigidarium* of the western baths supported the wall of the new building, and also the weight of its roof. On the north side, the Romans had made the wall very wide in anticipation of the downward thrust of the roof. The thicker wall served its purpose for a while but eventually it had to be buttressed. This was not done by simply adding massive pilasters to the outside of the wall, which would scarcely have been aesthetically pleasing to the eye, but by creating a portico all along it, with two arches at either end that also served the purpose of buttresses.[25] The western arch was open, but the other at the eastern end was probably a blind arch because it was contiguous with the precinct wall, and there is no evidence that an opening through the wall was ever placed here. In the centre of the portico a porch was built around the doorway leading into the pool, with four arches at right angles to each other, one set defining the route into and out of the building and the other set allowing access along the wall, matching up with the other two buttress-arches.

The façade of the enclosed pool, facing north into the temple precinct, was monumental and elaborate. The porch in the centre had a pitched roof and a triangular pediment above the entrance. Some of the sculptures that probably belonged to it have survived. One of the stones was found in 1790 but has since been lost, and survives only as a drawing, which shows that the carving was a circular arrangement with three steeply pointed triangles radiating from its centre, reminiscent of the radiate crown worn by later Roman Emperors on their coin portraits.[26] Two other sculptures may belong to this scene. One shows the lower torso and thighs of a figure that was evidently braced to lean over to its left, and the second one shows the waist and thighs of a similar figure leaning to its right.[27] The whole scene has been interpreted as a depiction of the head of Sol, the sun god, in the centre of a disc held aloft by two water nymphs, one on either side.[28]

Another Temple Opposite the Sacred Spring?

In 1790 when the Pump Room was being built, a carved head of a woman was found, depicted full face, with an elaborate hairstyle and a crescent behind her.[29] The stone belonged to a monument in the temple precinct, probably facing the porch of the enclosed sacred pool. It is broken in two and nothing is visible of the lady's hands, but over her left shoulder a whip is shown, which she presumably held in her left hand. It is suggested that she held the reins of her chariot, not visible, in her right hand, and that she is Luna, or goddess of the moon. This discovery has led to the suggestion that there was a deliberate juxtaposition of the porch with the representation of the sun god facing north, and the moon goddess opposite him on some unknown building facing south.

The goddess Luna may have belonged to a series of sculptures that have been labelled the Four Seasons, and a collection of fluted pilasters that were clearly not rounded columns but set against a wall. Nineteen sculptured fragments[30] and two inscriptions[31] were found at various times over two centuries from 1790 to 1982. An ingenious reconstruction shows a building façade divided into five sections, defined by six pilasters.[32] The central panel would have been a doorway and the two flanking panels on each side probably held the sculptured cupids, each with the attributes of one of the four seasons; flowers for spring, corn for summer, fruit for autumn and a bill hook for winter. This kind of theme is found in several floor mosaics with the seasons depicted as four people in each of the four corners, all bearing similar seasonal attributes.

The carved head of Luna would probably have been placed in the pediment above the panels. This reconstruction remains conjectural because no actual building is known on the north side of the temple precinct, facing the enclosed sacred pool. The absence of evidence does not necessarily mean that no building existed. There may have been a temple to Luna, or there may have simply been a false façade and no building behind it. Until some evidence comes to light, categorically disproving the theory, the opposition of the god of the sun and the goddess of the moon on either side of the precinct of the temple of Sulis Minerva, is the most plausible interpretation.

Other Public Buildings: the Theatre and the *Tholos*

Though at present there is no certain evidence for a theatre at Bath, the presence of such a building in the religious centre, close to the temple of Sulis Minerva, would not be out of place. In Greek tradition, a theatre was commonly built close by the temple and usually on the same alignment with it, and was used for religious performances. Two sites have been proposed for the conjectural theatre at Bath.[33] One is north of the temple, where the ground slopes steeply upwards, which would provide a good location for a theatre, using the natural contours of the land as support for the seating, just as happened in Greece where theatres are situated in a hollow of a hillside. There is no proof that a theatre existed here, but massive foundations were found in 1997 at the junction of Westgate Street and Union Street, and at a find spot near to Westgate Street, four large, sculpted blocks were found, belonging to the cornice of a building that would have been even larger than the temple. Taken together, these archaeological discoveries suggest that something large and important had been built here, and it may well be that it was a theatre.

The second postulated site for the theatre is in the area to the east of the temple precinct, and just to the north of the baths, where large foundation walls were discovered, on plan like a large letter 'E' lying on its side with three projecting longer walls running northwards. This is the only section that could be excavated, so it is not known how far to the north the excavated walls would have run. Since the full extent of the building that rested on these foundations could not be ascertained, it is not possible to be certain that a theatre was built here.

Alternatively the excavators suggested that these E-shaped foundation walls could have been part of another religious precinct. Between the foundations and the Great Bath, several sections of sculpted stone were found in the years 1878 to 1882. Four of these had clearly belonged to the top sections of a circular building. Three sections of a column, and two parts of a Corinthian capital, were found on a separate occasion. The column or columns presumably did not stand alone, but most probably belonged to the postulated *tholos*, which is a Greek term for a circular building. Though the existence of such a circular building is definitely attested, its location is not. Current thinking places it inside the western end of the abbey, standing inside a square or rectangular precinct which most likely married up with the precinct of the Temple of Sulis Minerva further west.[34]

Residential Buildings and Workshops

From time to time over many years, buildings have been discovered in various parts of Bath with painted walls and mosaic floors. It is unfortunate that hardly any of these buildings could be fully excavated, so archaeologists are left with pieces of a jigsaw for which they have no box lid with the complete picture. In most of the buildings there are not enough clues to suggest that they were houses owned and lived in by residents of Bath, or staff who worked at various jobs in the town, or whether they were part of the accommodation for visitors. Presumably the town was equipped with all these types of establishments.

Assuming that some of the buildings were houses for residents, it seems on present evidence that the north-west area of the town was the place to be.[35] On the site of the United Hospital, a house was discovered that had at least seven rooms, and probably more that were not revealed. In 1738, on the site of the Mineral Water Hospital another town house was found with a corridor with a mosaic floor, and a room leading off it, at least 5 metres across, which had another mosaic floor. Another room had a hypocaust supported on pillars, with a vent to take the heat to the next room, and a stone-flagged floor was discovered that may have been a courtyard. Nearby, in 1859, another house was found with a mosaic floor, part of which survives in the basement of the Mineral Water Hospital. This is where the fragment of white marble with the Sollemnis inscription[36] was found, together with pottery and coins, but the editors of *Roman Inscriptions in Britain* suggested that the Sollemnis inscription was a stray piece that did not necessarily belong to the other finds on this spot. The mosaics of sea creatures on display in the Roman Baths Museum came from a house on the site of the Bluecoat School, and two more mosaics were found on Bridewell Lane and the junction with this road and Westgate Street. This north-west area suggests affluence, but it is still not certain whether the buildings housed residents or visitors.

On the west side of the town, a house labelled the Citizen House[37] was partially excavated in 1964 and 1970. It had started out as a timber house, with painted walls, superseded by a stone-built version, also with painted walls, but it seems to have been converted into a workshop sometime later, where iron working was carried out. New floors were laid in this building, which continued in occupation until the fourth century.

In the south-west area, there were buildings associated with the Hot Bath springs, and the Cross Bath spring was enclosed within an oval wall. Buildings were discovered nearby but only sections of them were revealed and there was insufficient evidence as to their usage. Under Bellott's Hospital there was a stone building with at least three phases. In its second version, there was a corridor running roughly north to south with rooms off to the west, and a smithy was established in one of the rooms.

The south-east quarter of Roman Bath has yielded somewhat contradictory evidence of occupation.[38] In one of the cellars of the Crystal Palace pub in Abbey Green, part of a mosaic floor was found when alterations were being carried out, and to the north of it archaeologists discovered evidence of a continued series of demolition and rebuilding all dated to Roman times, leaving a metre of occupation debris under the house with the mosaic floor. On stylistic grounds the mosaic was dated to the second century, and on top of it a mortar floor had been laid, with fragments of third- and fourth-century pottery.

On the other hand there seems to have been little development in other parts of the south-east area of the town until the third century AD. North of Abbeygate Street and near the junction with Swallow Street, evidence of lead working was discovered, and a large stone building of the later third century with a range of rooms leading off a corridor. By the fourth century, one of the rooms had acquired a hypocaust and painted walls, and a separate house was located nearby also with painted walls. Later in the fourth century the buildings collapsed and were not rebuilt.

Large areas of Roman Bath remain unexplored, and can only be investigated when demolition of old structures takes place in advance of new building. It cannot be assumed that the whole of the town within the walls was fully occupied. In some of the towns of Roman Britain it has been discovered that some plots were never built on, as though the full potential of the town was over-estimated by the planners, or in some cases, areas devastated by fire or some calamity were never reclaimed. Aquae Sulis was smaller than most Romano-British towns, and as a religious centre and tourist attraction it probably held more visitors than residents at any one time, and the numbers of visitors may have fluctuated with the seasons.

Goddesses and Gods

The number of altars and other inscriptions dedicated to Sulis or Sulis Minerva clearly indicate that Sulis was the chief deity worshipped at Bath. Sulis is unknown in other areas, but Celtic gods and goddesses are usually of purely local origin with individual names, even if their attributes are shared with other deities.

The Romans did not usually try to suppress other religions, unless they felt that there was a threat to state security. Their objections to the Druidical cults of Gaul and Britain are obscured by hyperbole and lurid accounts of horrid barbarous practices, but these objections may have been political rather than religious, and may have arisen because the Druids could possibly have united otherwise disparate tribes in opposition to Rome. At a later time, the Christians too were seen as forming a state within a state, refusing to take the oath of loyalty to the Emperors over and above their loyalty to their god. Only in the fourth century was it realised that people could be loyal to both heavenly deity and earthly ruler, rendering unto Caesar, etc. etc., as had been stated about 300 years earlier.

In Roman Britain, as elsewhere in the Empire, the local gods and goddesses were usually equated with Roman deities whose attributes and powers were similar. The process of amalgamation, called syncretism, allowed worship to be carried out according to native and Roman forms. Sulis was equated with Minerva, the Roman goddess of arts and crafts, of wisdom, healing, and warfare.[39]

Minerva was one of the most important deities of Rome, one of the Capitoline Triad, the three major deities of the Roman world: Jupiter, his consort Juno and Minerva herself. As goddess of wisdom and warfare, Minerva shared her attributes with the important Greek goddess Athena, and like Athena, she is usually depicted with a helmet and breastplate and sometimes a spear, signifying her warlike aspects. The gilt-bronze head of Minerva, found in 1790 and displayed in the Roman Baths Museum, is now without a helmet, but the form of the casting indicates that she was originally provided with one, which makes it certain that it is the head of Minerva. There is little doubt that this head is part of the cult statue of Minerva that would once have been inside the temple, but no trace of a gilt-bronze body to go with it has been found.

Another of Minerva's attributes is wisdom, and to signify this aspect she is usually shown with an owl, like Athena. The symbols of Minerva are carved on the pediment of the temple of Sulis Minerva. There were probably two helmets at the base of the pediment, but only the one on the left survives. On the right it is probable that there was a second helmet, a mirror image of the extant one, and on top of this stands Minerva's owl, tucked away wearing a somewhat disgruntled expression, at the bottom-right-hand edge of the wreath surrounding the head of the so-called Gorgon.

The Gorgon's head usually appears on Minerva's shield or breastplate. A sculptured stone showing Minerva was found in the Great Bath in 1882, showing her with helmet, spear and shield, and wearing a depiction of the Gorgon's head across her torso.[40]

This association with the Gorgon is why the splendidly carved head in the centre of the pediment of the temple of Sulis Minerva has acquired the name. Since the Gorgons of Greek myth were indisputably female, and the carved head has moustaches and is obviously male, the head has also acquired the names of Neptune or Oceanus. At Chichester, a temple was built on the authority of Tiberius Claudius Togidubnus to Minerva and Neptune, so the Oceanus/Neptune label for the Gorgon's head could be related to this pairing of the goddess of war with the god of the oceans. The connection with the sea is perhaps supported by the appearance of Tritons, each with a human body and a fish tail, at each corner of the pediment, and the extant helmet on the pediment is fashioned in the shape of a dolphin. It is possible that all these figures convey the idea of the sea or flowing water, as perhaps represented by the flowing hair of the Gorgon.[41]

The hair of the Gorgon has also been seen as tongues of flame, representing the sun, and a possible connection with the goddess Sul/Sulis or the god Sol. There is some debate about the form of the name Sulis, which on first sight is similar to a Latin genitive form, so Aquae Sulis could mean that the true name of the goddess was Sul, converted into a Latinised genitive form as Sulis, meaning 'of Sul'. However, this is unlikely. Up to now no inscription has come to light recording the nominative form Sul; she is always Sulis. The similarity of the postulated name Sul to the Roman sun god Sol implies that there may have been some connection between them, but linguistically this is not necessarily the case.[42] One major objection to this theory is that Sulis is female and Sol is male. This combination of male and female elements in one figure is exactly what is argued for the so-called Gorgon's head on the pediment of the temple of Sulis Minerva, but this in no way supports the suggestion that the goddess Sulis and the god Sol are to be similarly equated.

Behind the Gorgon's head, partly obscured by the hair, there are traces of wings, and underneath the chin there are entwined snakes. This supports the suggestion that the head is that of a female Gorgon complete with snakes, but depicted in male form, thus neatly uniting male and female deities and also classical and native religious symbolism. Is the Gorgon intended to convey the idea of Minerva and also Sulis, combined into one single sculpture? The short answer is that there is no absolute consensus as to what it represents, but there is general agreement that the so-called Gorgon's head from Bath is one of the finest sculptures in Roman Britain. Comparison with another similar head with flowing hair and moustaches, from York, demonstrates very clearly the skill and sophisticated artistry of the sculptor of the Gorgon's head at Bath. The York example[43] is considered to portray a Celtic god, staring at the viewer, with prominent eyes and a drooping moustache, the whole head surrounded by waving locks. It is very worn, so that much of the detail is obscured, but although it is very similar to the Gorgon's head from the temple of Sulis Minerva, it was never so sharply depicted, and is much less 'alive'.

Sulis, as the most important and powerful goddess at Bath, is sometimes cited on her own, and sometimes in conjunction with Minerva, but up to now there is little evidence that she was usually addressed as Minerva Sulis, with the powerful Roman goddess given precedence.[44] People dedicated altars to Sulis, or set up statues in her honour. They gave her items of jewellery and everyday domestic implements, and thousands of coins, deposited in the sacred springs. Several of these items can be seen in the Roman Baths Museum.

The donation of these gifts was part of the contract between people and the goddess. The gifts may have been made when people asked favours of her in the hope of a successful outcome, or perhaps after a favourable result for which they wished to thank her. The requests were probably not exclusive to their state of health, but would have been made in all circumstances where they needed help, possibly not even for themselves but on behalf of someone else who was in difficulties. They sought her assistance and protection when wrongs had been done to them, as attested by the numbers of leaden curse tablets deposited in the sacred spring asking for redress, return of stolen goods or punishment of the malefactors. This is the darker side of Sulis; in the interests of justice she was sometimes asked to inflict extremely bloodthirsty retribution on guilty parties.

It is perhaps surprising that at such an important and long-lived healing centre there is no direct evidence of healing. There are several tombstones and therefore some incontrovertible evidence of deaths, though this does not necessarily mean that all attempts at cures were failures. The number of inscriptions recording the willing and deserved fulfilment of a vow, abbreviated to 'V.S.L.M.', standing for *votum solvit libens merito*, 'willingly and deservedly fulfilled his/her vow', may mean that some prayers for healing were answered. This must remain a theory, because people generally did not record what they had asked for from the gods, probably much like the taboo on revealing what was wished for when two people hook their little fingers around one section of the wish-bone of the chicken at special dinners, and pull the bones apart. For those not familiar with the custom, the person who ends up with the greater part of the wish-bone will have their request granted.

Not all of these 'V.S.L.M.' inscriptions from Bath were dedicated to Sulis, and it is also quite likely some of the vows made by individuals were completely unconnected with seeking a cure for some physical illness or mental turmoil. But even if every single inscription that was ever set up in Aquae Sulis still survived, the total would probably represent only a small percentage of the people who came to the springs. It is fairly certain that only wealthy individuals could afford to pay for an inscription on stone. Many more people must have attended the healing springs without leaving any record behind them, and many of them probably went home again satisfied with the results of their visit. People came to Bath from other towns of Roman Britain, and even from other provinces, so if no-one ever came away feeling slightly better than they did when they arrived, it is permissible to wonder why rumours of failure did not spread, and why the temple and baths of Aquae Sulis not only survived, but flourished, for nearly three centuries.

A variety of other gods and goddesses were worshipped at Bath besides Sulis Minerva. They are attested by artistic representations or by inscriptions naming them, though it is not always possible to link the epigraphic evidence with the sculptural portrayals. The figures on the altar that stood before the temple of Sulis Minerva have been identified as Bacchus, Jupiter, Hercules Bibax and possibly Apollo.[45] The other figures are too worn to identify them, but include a goddess bearing a cornucopia and pouring a libation from a vessel. Only three of the postulated four stones clasping the altar have been found, so it is not possible to say which other gods and goddesses were depicted on the fourth stone. The surviving representations are all classical deities of the Roman or Greek world, and so far none of them are represented in the collection of inscriptions that have been found. It is possible that, throughout the year, religious ceremonies were conducted at Aquae Sulis in honour of each of the gods depicted on the altar. Minerva's most ancient celebration was on 19 March, originally associated with the opening of the campaigning season for the Republican Roman army, though it is not known if this date was also celebrated at Bath.

The goddess Diana is represented at Bath by an inscription[46] found in the ruins of the Hot Bath in 1776. It was set up by a freedman called Vettius Benignus. The extant first line begins with '… NA', which does not make sense on its own, so it is suggested that the line above it was smoothed off, thus removing the letters 'DEA DIA …', which joined up with the second line to read 'the goddess Diana'. No other inscription mentioning Diana is known from Bath, but in 1982 a section of a sculptured stone was found in the temple precinct, where it had been ignominiously used as paving. It shows a finely carved dog, and a glimpse of someone behind the animal with a bow and arrow, interpreted as the huntress Diana with her hound.[47]

Somewhere in Bath, not as yet located, there was a temple to the god Mars. The only mention of it so far is on a lead curse tablet, recording a gift to the temple by a lady called Basilica.[48] Mars is also mentioned on an inscription found at the lower end of Stall Street in 1753.[49] This inscription was set up in honour of Loucetius Mars and the goddess Nemetona by Peregrinus, a citizen of the Treveri, whose capital was at Trier. The name Nemetona is derived from a Gallic word meaning a sacred place[50] and is related to *nemeton*, meaning shrine. The Roman name for the hot springs at Buxton, Aquae Arnemetiae, derives from the same source. In the Rhineland, the pairing of Loucetius Mars and

Nemetona is not uncommon, so Peregrinus adhered to the cult of his homeland while visiting or possibly even residing in Bath. The inscription records that he willingly and deservedly fulfilled his vow, so he had asked for some favour from his native gods and been satisfied with the result, which may or may not have been a cure for some malady.

There may be a depiction of Loucetius Mars and Nemetona at Bath. At an unrecorded site, a sculptured stone[51] that was found in the excavations of 1878–90 shows two figures. A male god stands on the right, wearing a short cloak and a horned helmet. He carries a purse in his right hand and a caduceus over his left shoulder. On the left is a female deity, who appears to be sitting down with her skirt spread over her knees and a box of some sort at her right side. The identification of the two figures as Loucetius Mars and Nemetona is not certain, and there is nothing to prove that the sculpture is in any way associated with Peregrinus from Trier, but on the other hand the pairing of a god and a goddess on the same stone makes it likely that these two deities are represented here.

At the base of this sculpture there is an animal of indeterminate species, and three cloaked figures, too worn to show much detail. These may be intended to show the *genii cucullati*, three minor deities who may be associated with fertility, wealth, and general well-being. The *cucullati* are usually shown wearing all-enveloping cloaks with hoods, called *cuculli*, from which the deities derive their name. These figures, always in threes, are common in Gaul, Germany and Britain, and most especially in Gloucestershire. In some cases in the Roman Empire the three hooded figures are accompanied by an inscription specifically naming them as *genii cucullati*. There are sculptural examples of these deities in the

Roman Museum at Cirencester, one finely carved, and another is rendered in the most schematic fashion, showing angular outlines with no attempt to provide realistic detail. There is another famous depiction of the three *cucullati* at Housesteads fort on Hadrian's Wall. Their cloaks cover them so completely that only their faces and feet are shown. On the stone at Bath, probably depicting Loucetius Mars and Nemetona, the identification of the three figures as *cucullati* is supported by the association of these deities with healing springs, as at Springhead in Kent.

The number three has special significance in Celtic religion, and the *cucullati* are often associated with the mother goddesses, the *Deae Matres*, also grouped in threes. Like the *cucullati*, the three mother goddesses are common in Gaul, Germany and Britain, on sculptured stones that vary in artistic quality. At Bath, the three highly schematic figures that on first sight look like visiting extra-terrestrials, with stem-like necks and bulging eyes, may represent the mother goddesses. They wear pleated skirts and have their arms folded across their chests. There are no inscriptions or associated finds to explain what they represent, but the absence of hooded cloaks precludes their identification as *cucullati*, and their skirts marking them as female support the suggestion that they are mother goddesses.

Worship of the three mother goddesses, or at least an aspect of them, is attested at Bath by a dedication to the Suleviae, found at the lower end of Stall Street in 1753.[52] The Suleviae are specifically designated as mother goddesses on an inscription from Colchester, dedicated by Similis, son of Attus, to the *matres Suleviae* in fulfilment of a vow.[53] The altar at Bath was set up by Sulinus, the son of Brucetus, who describes himself as a sculptor. This same man set up another inscription to the Suleviae at Cirencester[54] in fulfilment of a vow. The stone was found in the north-west quarter of Cirencester in 1899, together with two other sculptured reliefs, each showing three mother goddesses. Another fragmentary inscription mentioning the Suleviae was found beyond the site of the south gate of Cirencester.[55] The only other location where an altar to the Suleviae has been found is at the fort at Binchester, dedicated by an unknown person of the *ala Vettonum*.[56] The stone, or rather the broken fragment, was discovered in 1760, and a record of the decipherable lettering was made, but apart from this record there is now no trace of the original stone. The supposition that the abbreviation starting with 'SUL ...' refers to the Suleviae is not absolutely certain, but the soldiers stationed at Binchester made five other dedications to the *matres*, the mother goddesses. Together with the dedication to the Suleviae, this constitutes six mother goddess inscriptions out of the total of thirteen that were found at the fort before the mid-1960s.

The cavalry unit of the Vettones is attested on other inscriptions from the fort at Binchester, and it may be significant that a trooper from this same unit, Lucius Vitellius Tancinus,[57] died at Bath aged forty-six, having joined the unit aged twenty and served for twenty-six years. The stone can be seen in the Roman Baths Museum. The top of the sculptured relief is missing, but the lower part of the depiction of Tancinus is still visible. He is shown mounted on his horse, riding to the right over a defeated enemy lying below the horse's hooves.[58] This is a standardised pose for the tombstones of Roman cavalrymen all over the Empire.

Tancinus came from Caurium in Lusitania, the homeland of the Vettones. Since it is known that, as soon as a province was stabilised sufficiently, Roman army units regularly recruited men from the local areas where they were stationed rather than the original tribesmen for whom the unit is named, the presence of a native of the Vettones in the cavalry unit at Bath has been taken to indicate that Tancinus died not too long after the unit was formed. He may have been one of the first recruits. If so, this tombstone dates from the very early period of Roman Britain, set up at a time when the unit still retained some of its native Lusitanian tribesmen. It has been dated to the late Claudian or early Neronian period, possibly around the late AD 50s, before the baths and temple of Sulis Minerva were constructed. The Vettones could have been stationed at the postulated early fort at Bath. Perhaps the cavalry unit was familiar with the hot springs nearby, and adopted the gods and goddesses of the area, still remembering them corporately when they moved to other forts.

Other religious inscriptions from Aquae Sulis include a dedication to the spirit of the place or *genius loci*, and to the *numen Augusti*, the spirit of the Emperor. The English translation 'spirit' does not quite convey the full meaning of *numen* or *genius*. Dedications to the *genius loci* are common in Roman Britain, to propitiate the deity who presided over the area, or to give thanks for help received. Only one survives from Bath, an altar dedicated by a soldier of the VI legion, called Forianus or perhaps Torianus.[59]

The worship of the Roman Emperors represented different ideas to the people of the eastern and western provinces. In the east, worship of the king or leader himself as a god on earth was quite normal and perfectly acceptable, but in the west, especially in Rome itself, the worship of a living individual was abhorrent. Instead of worship of a living Emperor, the Imperial cult was designed for worship of the spiritual power or the divine will of the gods, which the Emperor embodied within his lifetime. This divorced the living man from his divine attributes and made worship of the Emperor acceptable in the west. After death, Emperors could be deified, becoming real gods, unless they had been particularly objectionable in life, like Nero or Domitian, and then the process of deification was not carried out.

Probably in the AD 160s, Gaius Curiatius Saturninus, a centurion of II Augusta, dedicated an altar to Sulis Minerva and to the spirits of two Emperors ruling together.[60] This is indicated by the abbreviation 'AUGG' on the inscription. When only one Emperor is meant, 'AUG' is used; two Emperors merit an additional letter 'G' and three Emperors are represented by three letter 'G's. It is suggested that this particular inscription dates from some time during the joint reigns of Marcus Aurelius and Lucius Verus, AD 161 to 169. Curiatius Saturninus had made a vow to set up an altar to these deities, on behalf of himself and his family (*pro se siusque*), for whom he had probably asked a favour. The stone can be seen in the Roman Baths Museum. It was found in the cistern of the Cross Bath, so if the dedication was actually made at the Cross Bath, it is possible that a member of Saturninus's family had found relief there from some complaint.

Another dedication to 'the spirit and virtue' of the Emperor[61] was made by Gaius Severius Emeritus, who was *centurio regionarius*, or centurion in charge of the region. The stone was found in 1753 in Stall Street, and is now in the Roman Baths Museum. The inscription records the fact that some part of the holy place (*locus religiosus*), or something located there, had been destroyed and had been restored and cleansed, probably in the religious sense of re-sanctifying the place or the monument. No certain date can be ascribed to the impious destruction, or to the work of Severius Emeritus in clearing it up, but the inscription reveals that vandalism is not a new phenomenon.

There are probably many more religious dedications, inscriptions and sculptures awaiting discovery at Bath, perhaps including other gods not represented on the extant stones. From the collection so far assembled, it is clear that although Sulis can be said to preside over the religious complex and all three of the hot springs, it was possible to venerate other gods and ask favours of them at all the sacred locations. The inscription cited above, recording some destruction at Aquae Sulis which was repaired by Emeritus, may imply that practitioners of the cults of the different gods and goddesses did not always live harmoniously with each other, but in general there was probably a wider degree of tolerance between worshippers than there is in the modern world.

Part of the relationship between people and the gods was similar to a business contract. Prayers could be addressed to an individual god, with an immediate offering for the temple, or the promise of some future service to be performed in return for a favourable result, such as setting up an altar to the god or goddess in question if the prayer was answered successfully. This is why so many people in the Roman world proclaim that their altar was set up as fulfilment of a vow, the formulaic phrase that expresses this, *votum solvit libens merito*, being reduced to its initials 'V.S.L.M.' or a variant form expressing the same sentiments, common enough to be instantly understood. There was no need to maintain undivided loyalty to one specific deity, especially since each god or goddess possessed particular attributes and powers over various aspects of life. According to the problem that was to be solved, it was advisable to ask the most appropriate god or goddess for help, and the prayer could be for something rather frivolous, not necessarily limited to matters of life and death, health, wealth and prosperity. As stated above, people did not usually include on the dedicatory inscription what they had asked for, but in the northern part of Roman Britain, in what is now the county of Durham, at least one man, Gaius Tetius Veturius Micianus, prefect of the *ala Sebosiana*, was willing to spend money on a joyful and garrulously boastful dedication to the god Silvanus, a nature god presiding over fields and woods, the most appropriate deity to help Veturius Micianus obtain what he desired. With the help of the god Silvanus, Micianus had successfully hunted a splendid wild boar that nobody else had managed to kill.[62]

The Curse Tablets

An additional form of the relationship between humans and gods is illustrated by the lead curse tablets found at Bath and other Romano-British sites. This is an established Graeco-Roman custom not limited to Britain. People who had been wronged in some way could ask the god or goddess to curse the person or persons they held responsible for whatever transgressions had been made against them. The procedure was to outline the problem and also the preferred remedy by inscribing the details on a sheet of lead or pewter, and then to roll it up, or less often leave it flat, to be placed in the appropriate location in or near a shrine, or buried in the earth, or placed inside a tomb, or nailed to a tree. These curse tablets were called *defixiones* in Latin, and a large quantity of such tablets were found in the sacred spring at Bath.[63]

The *defixiones* may not have been the only way of obtaining divine justice and retribution. It is quite possible that some of the altars that were dedicated to various gods in fulfilment of a vow also concerned a prayer for help with regard to injuries to people or their relatives, or to their property, without actually recording any details in the text. Given the choice of waiting for a request to be answered and then putting up an inscribed stone, or having an altar produced in anticipation of a favourable result, the preparation of a *defixio* was probably more immediate, more private and personal, more satisfying as a way of dissipating anger, and at the same time less cumbersome, and most of all less expensive. Predominantly it was the poorer people who utilised *defixiones* to try to recoup their losses and gain revenge. It would have been long-winded and expensive to go to the law, perhaps risking a failure to obtain justice in the end, and in any case the curse tablets are full of mere suspicions rather than ascertainable facts. Much of the time the wronged person did not truly know who was the guilty party, so rather than remain helpless, he or she could act almost immediately and at little expense, to ask the god or goddess for help, because the gods knew the inmost secrets of all people, and would know who to blame.

Lead curse tablets are not confined to Bath. At the shrine at Uley in Gloucester there were at least 140 of them, spread all over the temple precincts rather than concentrated in one special place.[64] There may be still more to find, at Uley and at Bath. Others have been found at London and Caerleon. What the tablets reveal, among other things, is that there was a flourishing trade in stolen goods at Bath, in particular items of clothing such as expensive cloaks with hoods, lost by at least three people. Among other items of clothing stolen at Bath there are two shirts, two bath-robes, called *balneares*, a pair of gloves, a headband and an ordinary cloak.[65] Attending the baths without accompanying friends or slaves to watch over personal possessions meant that one's discarded clothing was at the mercy of thieves, and given the expensive nature of some British woollens, renowned in the Empire, the highest prices could presumably be obtained for a fine hooded cloak on the streets of Bath itself, probably five minutes down the road after stealing it. As with any tourist resort, the visitors who were unfortunate victims of theft would have less chance of finding the culprits, so there may have been several regular receivers of stolen goods in Aquae Sulis and other towns. In Roman times as well as nowadays, good fences did not always make good neighbours.

The losses sustained by many of the victims were not confined to the baths. Stolen pots and pans are mentioned, which probably means that the thief entered the house, rather than that he stole the kitchen equipment that had been left as part of the shopping while the victim was at the baths. Theft of money is also recorded on more than one curse tablet, and possibly even theft or abduction of wives or girlfriends, if this is what is meant by the name Vilbia on the most frequently quoted example of a curse tablet from Bath.[66] The person who wrote this curse asks that whoever carried off Vilbia should become 'liquid as water'. Since Vilbia is a feminine form of name, it was considered that the curse must be about the loss of a girlfriend, but more recently doubt has been cast on the identity of Vilbia. Perhaps this is not a person at all. It has been suggested that Vilbia was a bath towel. The fact that the text implies that he, she, or it, was 'consumed' might even suggest that an animal had been spirited away, like a prized pig reduced to pork. No-one knows.

But whatever Vilbia was, the tablet illustrates several features of curses. The words are inscribed in the right order, but the letters of each word are written backwards. Several suspects are named, and the suppliant, whoever he or she may be, asks that these people should be struck dumb. Some of the punishments that are sought can be extremely gory, possibly reflecting the degree of anger experienced by the victim; for instance Dicomedis lost a pair of gloves, and asked that whoever stole them should lose his mind and his eyes. A frequent request was that the wrongdoer should never sleep. With a little imagination, this is probably worse, and certainly more prolonged, than being turned to liquid.

Although the curse tablets were placed in the sacred spring of Sulis, the formula used in the text does not always mention Sulis by name. There was probably no need to name her because, being a goddess, she would know that she had been asked for help, and she would also know who addressed her and why. Other victims would dedicate the stolen goods to the deity, or some other gift if the goods should be returned. Sometimes the culprit was given to the goddess as well, presumably for punishment.

Some of the curse texts are very brief, but others have obviously tried to cover all loopholes in asking for punishment of the unknown transgressors, by including all possible categories, whether man or woman, boy or girl, slave or free. This semi-legal formulaic terminology suggests that there were advisers on hand to assist with the composition of the curse, to make sure that nothing had been forgotten that might allow the wrongdoers to wriggle through the net and escape punishment. There would be a fee for this service. Some tablets from Uley and Bath imply that there was a fee for copying the text.[67]

The many curse tablets cannot necessarily be used to demonstrate the spread of literacy at Aquae Sulis. An examination of the individual styles of writing on the curse tablets shows that they varied in quality. Some of them are written in a practised hand, and may have been procured ready-made from an adviser, paid for by a person who was not literate. There may have been special premises, probably in the immediate vicinity of the baths, where these legal advisers had their offices, producing curse tablets as part of their wider legal businesses. The adviser would listen to the complaints, tease out the details, including names of suspects if any, and find out what the client really wanted to happen to the guilty party. Then the text would be composed, covering all possible types of perpetrators, probably read out to the client for approval, and then copied onto a lead sheet. The client could pay for the advice and also the lead sheet, and then take it away for deposit in the sacred spring. There may have been a fee for that, too.

Other curse tablets show varying degrees of literacy. Some of them were probably copied out by the victims themselves from a prepared text that had been written up for them, rather than purchasing a completed tablet composed and inscribed by a specialist. Then perhaps the prepared text on a writing tablet or vellum could be taken home and studied a few times in the hope of satisfaction, knowing that the lead version was safely with Sulis or another deity. Perhaps there was considerable satisfaction in writing the words on the lead tablet oneself, or perhaps there was greater religious force behind the curses if the wronged persons created the tablets by inscribing the words with their own hand. The standard of the writing on some of the tablets is very low, perhaps implying that one or two people who could not actually read and write, but wanted to produce their own curses, simply copied the shapes that had been written for them, rather than understanding what the letters meant.

As mentioned above, the curse tablets probably represent the poorer residents and visitors of Aquae Sulis. A curse is the last resort of the powerless. A wealthy person, with a household full of relatives, retainers, labourers and slaves, would perhaps not have bothered with an appeal to the gods, naming likely suspects on a *defixio*, but would simply have sent the boys round to the relevant address, where they might indulge in a spot of light chastisement.

5

BATH PEOPLE

The collection of people's names recorded on inscriptions and curse tablets presumably represents only a fraction of the residents and visitors who were connected with Roman Bath. Clearly there will have been some people who lived and worked in the town, and over the centuries there will have been many visitors who came for various reasons, perhaps on a pilgrimage, like Peregrinus, who felt obliged to inform people that he came from Trier.[1] Unfortunately on most inscriptions there is no mention of the place of origin of the person who erected the stones, and even if people did include this information there is still no way to distinguish between residents and visitors.

Among the people who left some record of themselves there are soldiers and civilians, slaves, freedmen and freedwomen, Roman citizens and non-citizens, artisans and tradesmen, rich and poor. The resident population of Roman Bath was perhaps only small compared to the numbers of visitors passing through, but someone must have lived in the town to provide the staff for the temple and the baths, and the service industries that went with them.

Religious Personnel

The temple of Sulis Minerva, and any other temples and shrines in Bath, would require a person or a group of people for their day-to-day running and maintenance. Only two inscriptions attest religious personnel, one being the tombstone of Gaius Calpurnius Receptus,[2] a priest of the goddess Sulis (*sacerdos deae Suli*), and the other a dedication to Sulis by the *haruspex*, Lucius Marcius Memor.[3] The tombstone of Receptus was found in 1795 near Sydney Gardens in the parish of Bathwick. Since Roman law sensibly forbade the burial of the dead inside the towns, tombstones are regularly found on the roads leading out of settlements. Calpurnia Trifosa, widow of Receptus, set up the stone, recording that Receptus had died aged 75, and that she had been his freedwoman and then his wife.

This is the only record of a priest of Sulis, but it can be safely assumed that there was a long line of priests serving the temple of the goddess, perhaps even a college of priests all serving together. There may have been someone on duty at all times, attending the sacred fire, which according to the ancient geographical writer Solinus[4] was never allowed to go out. Solinus does not mention Bath by name, but in connection with Britain he relates that at the temple of Minerva the perpetual fire does not produce white ash, but leaves rocky lumps when the flames die down, by which he presumably means cinders, indicating that the Romans burned coal at the temple. Somerset coal was abundant and easily extracted and was most likely used in the baths for heating the water and the hot room, and probably by residents who were fortunate enough to possess a hypocaust system. The use of coal in Roman Bath is attested by the discovery in 1867 of a pile of cinders in a corner of the temple precinct.[5]

The inscription recording the *haruspex* Lucius Marcius Memor was discovered underneath the Pump Room during the excavations in 1965. The inscribed stone most likely formed the base of a statue, and the carved text reveals that Marcius Memor had dedicated it as a gift to Sulis. The statue is not known, but more important than the statue is the title *haruspex* on the inscription. It was originally denoted by only three letters, 'HAR', beautifully centred, but at a later time '… USP' was added to make it clear what the abbreviation signified. It has been suggested that the title *haruspex* was not very well known in Britain[6] so explanation had to be proffered in the form of extra letters that spoiled the symmetry of the inscription. In the Roman world, the *haruspex* was an important member of the religious personnel, who divined the future and interpreted the will of the gods by examining the entrails of sacrificial animals. The literal and rather off-putting meaning of the word *haruspex* is gut-gazer, and the origin of the practice is probably Etruscan. The chief organ of divination was the liver and gallbladder of the sacrificed animal. The overall shape and the colour of the liver were important, but there was more to the proceedings than this, as implied by the discovery in parts of the Roman Empire of model livers made of metal, with various zones marked out on them. At Bath, people who had a problem, or were ill themselves, or had relatives who were suffering, would probably want to consult the *haruspex* to find out if the omens were favourable. Prediction of the future by looking at the livers of dead animals may seem bizarre, but before dismissing it out of hand it is perhaps worth a moment's reflection that it was probably just as successful for the punters, if somewhat more messy, as consulting a medium, or reading the Tarot cards, tea leaves or the I Ching.

Among the temple staff, there would have been people responsible for cleaning and general maintenance, and someone would have been responsible for procuring the fuel for the sacred fire, for storing it somewhere, and for overseeing the perpetual flame. The unfortunate people doing these dirty jobs would most likely have been slaves.

Running the Bathing Establishment

At the baths, there would have been a continuing need for fuel to heat the water in the boilers and maintain the under-floor heating for the hot rooms. Slaves would have performed the undesirable tasks of raking out the ashes and relighting the fires of the furnaces and the hypocausts. They may have been public slaves, owned corporately by the town, or they may have belonged to a private individual who ran the bathing facilities. It is thought that major bathing establishments belonged to the state, but even if they did, there would be a proprietor or contractor, usually termed a *conductor*, who would have paid out a lump sum for a contract to run the baths, probably for a specified fixed term, perhaps five or ten years.[7]

The *conductor* would then appoint the staff and oversee the running of the facilities. The baths must have consumed staggering quantities of fuel, probably using both wood and coal. The *conductor* and his staff would have to ensure that sufficient fuel was always on hand, and deal with the payments to whoever was supplying it. The furnaces would have to be checked several times

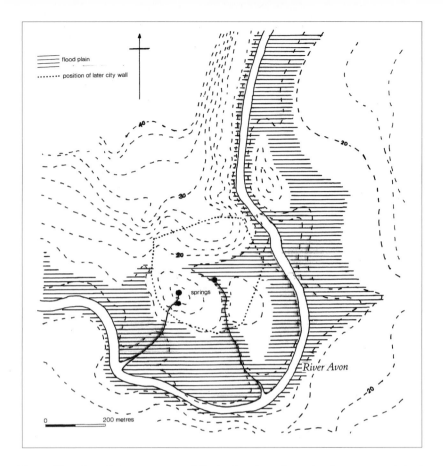

Above: Fig. 1. Site plan of the area around Bath, showing where the three vents of the hot springs emerge in relation to the later Roman walls. The River Avon loops around the town to the south and the ground rises steadily to the north. (Drawn by Jacqui Taylor after Cunliffe 2000)

Below: Fig. 2. Plan of Aquae Sulis showing the main temple area and the main baths complex, which together take up a large proportion of the town. The two other springs rise in the area to the left or west of the baths. The outline of what would become the Cross Bath is shaped like a spoon, and the Hot Bath was nearby. The Romans used all three springs. (Drawn by Jacqui Taylor after Cunliffe 2000)

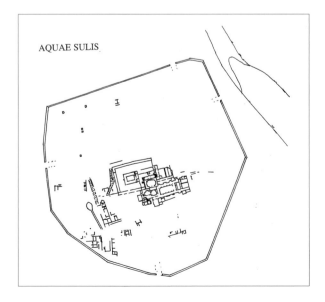

Above: Fig 3. Sketch plan of the centre of the modern city of Bath, with the Roman remains superimposed. The dates refer to excavations carried out in the areas so marked. (Drawn by Jacqui Taylor after Cunliffe 2000)

Opposite top: Fig. 4. A more detailed plan of the area around the Roman versions of the Cross Bath and the Hot Bath. (Drawn by Jacqui Taylor after Cunliffe 2000)

Opposite bottom: Fig. 5. Eighteenth-century plan of Bath, showing the King's Bath at 'A' and the Queen's Bath at 'B', almost in the centre of the town. The Cross Bath and the Hot Bath are respectively at 'C' and 'D', and to the west of these baths St John's Hospital at 'G'. The abbey is at 'I', labelled on the plan as St Peter's Cathedral. The Roman remains of the temple and main baths extended unseen and unknown from the abbey to the west side of Stall Street. (Drawn by Jacqui Taylor after Cunliffe 2000

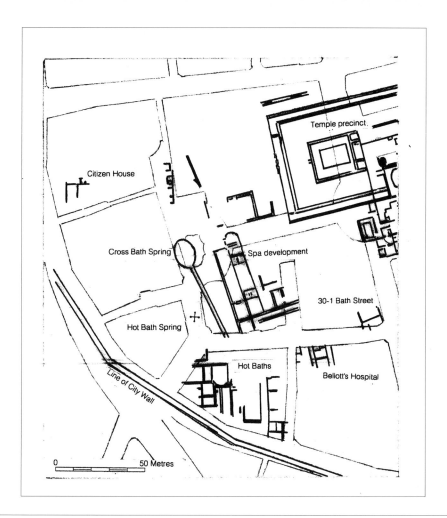

Temple precinct

Citizen House

Cross Bath Spring

Spa development

Hot Bath Spring

30-1 Bath Street

Line of City Wall

Hot Baths

Bellott's Hospital

0   50 Metres

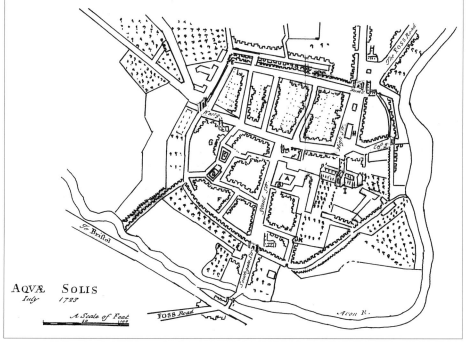

The FOSS Road

North G.

West G.

High Street

East G.

G

Paul St.

A

To Bristol

F

Southgate Str.

FOSS Road

Avon R.

AQVÆ SOLIS
Iuly 1723

A Scale of Feet
50   100

Fig. 6. Reconstruction of the façade of the temple of Sulis Minerva. The size of the eastern front is calculated from the probable extent of the pediment, which would allow for four columns, parts of which have been found, showing that they were of the Corinthian order with fluted columns and leafy capitals. Roman-style classical temples were not common in Roman Britain, and of those which have so far been discovered, the temple of Sulis Minerva is the only one for which there is such abundant evidence for its appearance and size. (Drawn by Jacqui Taylor after Cunliffe 2000)

Fig. 7. Drawing of the Gorgon's head from the temple pediment. There are wings behind the head, and snakes below the chin. The ideology of this vigorous portrait is still strongly debated. (Drawn by Jacqui Taylor)

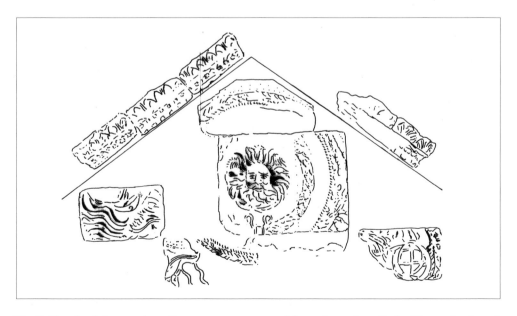

Fig. 8. Sketch of the temple pediment as reconstructed from the various finds. (Drawn by Jacqui Taylor)

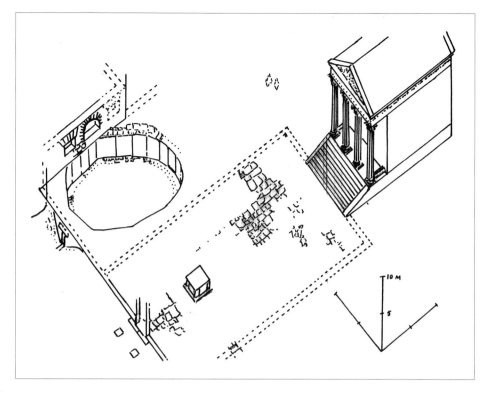

Fig. 9. The first version of the temple precinct and the open enclosure of the sacred spring. (Drawn by Jacqui Taylor after Cunliffe 2000)

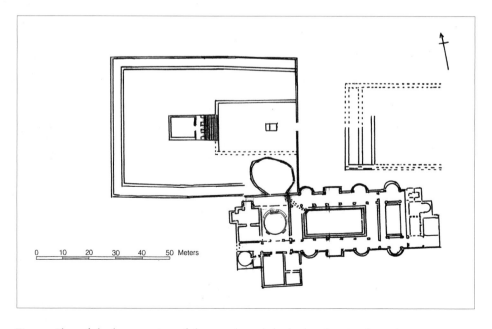

Fig. 10. Plan of the later version of the temple and the baths, showing how they were related to each other. The plan also shows the massive foundations of an unknown building to the east of the temple precinct. (Drawn by Jacqui Taylor after Cunliffe 2000)

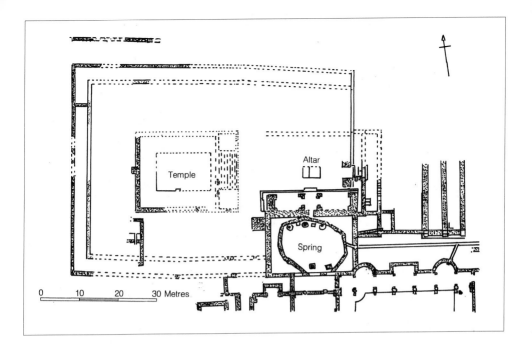

Above: Fig. 11. In its later phase the sacred spring was enclosed within a rectangular building with a vaulted roof. It projected further into the temple precinct, nearly to the altar. This plan shows how the outer wall to the north of the enclosed spring had to be buttressed to carry the weight of the roof, but in this case it was imaginatively done, with a porch in the centre over the entrance and two arches at right angles to the wall. (Drawn by Jacqui Taylor after Cunliffe 2000)

Right: Fig. 12. The inscription recording the *haruspex* Lucius Marcius Memor was found in 1965 during excavations in the cellars below the Pump Room. All those who regard archaeology as a romantic occupation might like to know that it was dug out of a somewhat aromatic sewer. (Drawn by Jacqui Taylor)

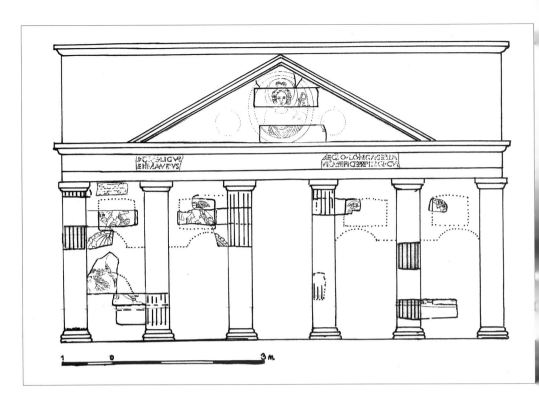

Above: Fig. 13. The so-called Façade of the Four Seasons. The several pieces of fluted columns, sculptured stones and two inscriptions that were found at various times are here reassembled in a reconstruction of either a decorated wall or possibly a building that was probably situated on the north side of the temple precinct, facing the sacred spring. The pediment of the façade shows a goddess with a crescent moon behind her head, interpreted as Luna, the goddess of the moon. It is conjectured that the pediment of the porch over the entrance to the sacred spring may have had a representation of the sun, so the two deities faced each other. (Drawn by Jacqui Taylor after Cunliffe 2000)

Left: Fig. 14. The two sculptured figures on the cornerstone of the altar in the temple precinct. This stone was discovered in 1790 and the two deities are interpreted as Jupiter, wearing his cloak, with an eagle to his left and Hercules Bibax, naked except for his lion skin with the forepaws knotted over his chest. (Drawn by Jacqui Taylor)

Above left: Fig. 15. Another corner of the altar was discovered in 1965. This one shows Bacchus, with the worn figure of a panther on his right and an unidentified goddess, who holds a cornucopia. (Drawn by Jacqui Taylor)

Above right: Fig. 16. Relief sculpture of Minerva that was found in the Great Bath. The goddess is identified by the Gorgon's head across her chest and stomach. She also has her helmet, and her owl is shown standing on her shield. (Drawn by Jacqui Taylor)

Right: Fig. 17. Relief sculpture of a god and a goddess. The stone was found at the end of the nineteenth century but it is not known exactly where it came from. The god with the horned, or winged, helmet may be Mercury, but it is also suggested that he is Leucetius, or Loucetius as he is known on the inscription set up by Peregrinus from Trier. If this is correct, then the female figure wearing a long skirt is probably Nemetona. Both deities were worshipped in Gaul and Germany. The three small, cloaked figures at the bottom have been interpreted as *genii cucullati*. (Drawn by Jacqui Taylor)

Above: Fig. 18. This stone probably represents the three mother goddesses, or an aspect of them. They are definitely female figures, judging by their pleated skirts. (Drawn by Jacqui Taylor)

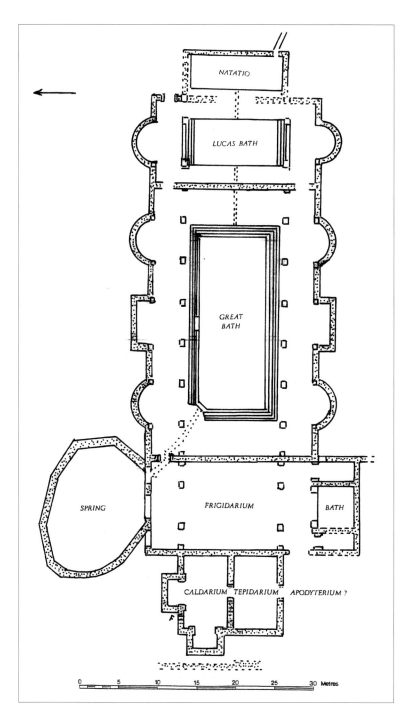

Fig. 19. This plan shows the first bathing establishment, which was a sophisticated building, but relatively simple compared to the increasing elaboration as time went on. The sacred spring is enclosed by a retaining wall to create the reservoir of hot water, but it is open to the sky, and can be viewed through the openings in the north wall of the entrance hall, labelled *frigidarium* or cold room. At the western end of the large bath, fed by the hot springs, there is a modest suite of conventional baths with a warm room (*tepidarium*) and hot room (*caldarium*), and a probable *apodyterium* or undressing room, at the south-west corner. The excavations of the baths have been impressive but the full extent of the building complex is still not known. (Drawn by Jacqui Taylor after Cunliffe 2000)

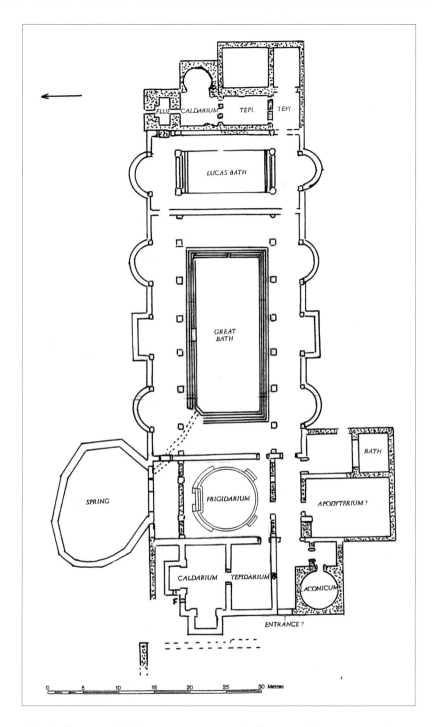

Fig. 20. The bathing establishment in its second phase. At the eastern end a new set of conventional baths has been built, replacing the former swimming pool or *natatio*. This probably indicates increased demand for services, and may be related to Hadrian's legislation which separated men and women at the baths, either by allocating separate opening hours or in some cases by adding new facilities. At the western end the baths have been extended southwards and more rooms added. The former *frigidarium* has been converted into the Circular Bath still visible today, and a hot room (*laconicum*) has been added. This was a dry hot room that worked like a sauna. (Drawn by Jacqui Taylor after Cunliffe 2000)

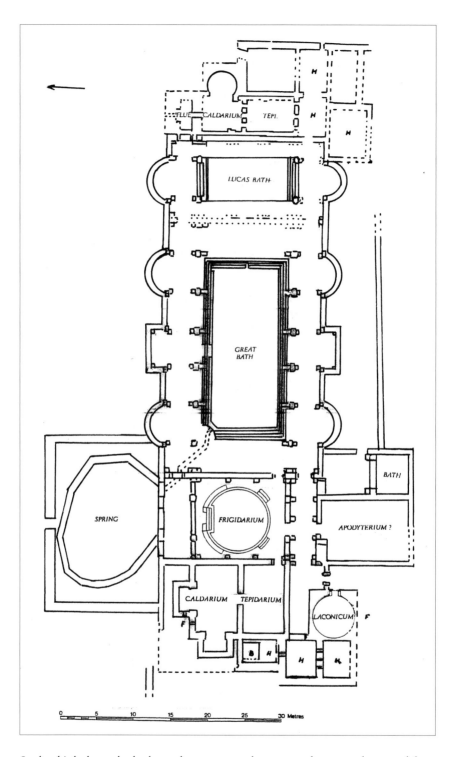

Fig. 21. In the third phase, the baths at the western and eastern ends are much more elaborate, with extra rooms added, and the sacred spring has been enclosed within a rectangular room with a vaulted roof. The Great Bath was probably roofed in wood at first, but in the third phase it received a vaulted roof running west to east. One of the supporting arches can still be seen at the baths, now at the level of the walkway. The concrete vault would be very heavy, and to support it the pillars running around the bath had to be strengthened. (Drawn by Jacqui Taylor after Cunliffe 2000)

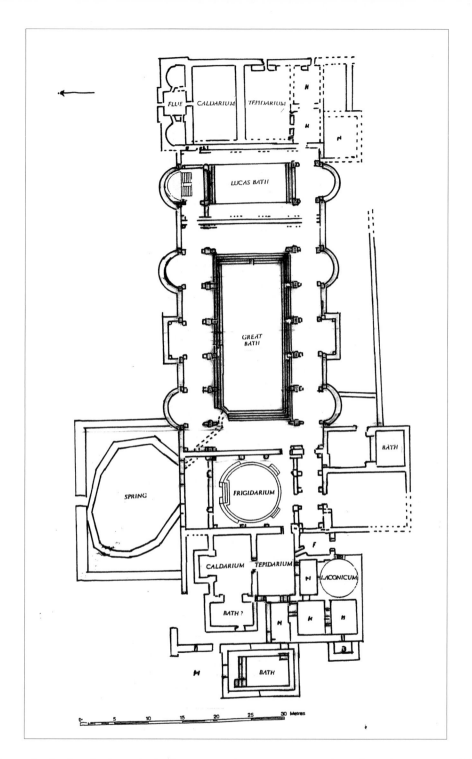

Fig. 22. In the fourth phase the baths were made even more complicated. At the eastern end the old *caldarium* and *tepidarium* were enlarged, with enhanced furnaces and flues, and a series of small hot rooms with hypocausts added. A cold bath was added to the northern end of the Lucas Bath. The western baths received more hot rooms and extensions were built further west. There may have been more rooms beyond the limits of the excavations. (Drawn by Jacqui Taylor after Cunliffe 2000)

The Inscriptions of Aquae Sulis

Up to 1965, all inscribed stones found on Romano-British sites are contained in *The Roman Inscriptions of Britain*, edited by R. G. Collingwood and R. P. Wright in 1965 and reissued in a new edition in 1995 with addenda and revisions by R. S. O. Tomlin. The selection included here covers most of the inscribed texts, with the exception of the fragmentary ones featuring only a few letters.

The lines of text on Roman inscriptions pay scant regard to punctuation, or to line-length, unless they are to be beautifully centred. The words are often split between lines without the benefit of a hyphen, as is customary in modern typesetting. Inscriptions also contain many abbreviations, which were more or less standard across the whole Roman Empire. Personal names were represented by their initials, 'M' standing for Marcus, 'L' for Lucius, 'G' or 'C' for Gaius or Caius, 'Ti' for Tiberius to distinguish it from 'T' for Titus. On tombstones, the letters 'D M' stand for *Dis Manibus*, meaning 'to the gods and shades' or the spirits of the dead, and 'H S E' stands for *hic situs est* or *hic sita est* for a woman, meaning 'he, or she, lies here'. 'H F C' stands for the phrase *heres faciendum curavit*, informing the viewer that the tombstone was set up by the appointed heir of the deceased.

In order to save space on the stone, and also to spare the stone-carver extra work, the letters are sometimes ligatured, so the letters 'I' and 'N' might appear on the stone as a capital 'N' with the left-hand or right-hand vertical stroke extended upwards, depending on whether the letter 'I' should occur before or after the letter 'N'. On a worn stone this practice can make it more difficult to read the inscription. On occasion the stones are damaged and some letters or even words and phrases are missing. Scholars can restore most of these lacunae, since many inscriptions are formulaic and it is sometimes possible to understand what would have been written in the missing sections. When inserting the absent letters or words into a transliteration of the inscription, the convention is to place these definite or hypothetical additions in square brackets, indicating that the letters or words are not actually visible on the stone. Curved brackets, on the other hand, are used to complete the abbreviated words, in the singular or plural, and with the correct Latin case ending, as demanded by the sense of the text, for instance where a genitive ending is called for, meaning 'of' something, or a dative ending, meaning giving something to someone. For the sake of simplicity in this list of inscriptions, the full restored Latin version is given without the hindrance of the multiplicity of brackets signifying gaps in the text or abbreviated forms. All the drawings are by Jacqui Taylor after Collingwood and Wright 1965.

There are two books which are useful in interpreting inscriptions:
Lawrence Keppie, *Understanding Roman Inscriptions* (Routledge, 2001).
John Rogan, *Reading Roman Inscriptions* (Tempus, 2006; History Press, 2010).

Fig. 23. This altar was found in Stall Street in 1922. It is a dedication to Sulis by the freedman of a standard-bearer of Legio II Augusta. The inscription is damaged and therefore has some gaps, which have been filled in by the editors of *Roman Inscriptions of Britain*. Though not all the letters are present, the text would have read in Latin as *Deae Suli ob salute sacrum Gai Iavoleni Saturnalis … imaginiferi legionis II Augustae Lucius Manius Dionisias libertus votum solvit libens merito*. 'To the goddess Sulis, for the welfare of Gaius Iavolenus Saturnalis … *imaginifer* of Legio II Augusta, Lucius Manius Dionisias, his freedman, willingly and deservedly fulfilled his vow.' (*RIB* I 147)

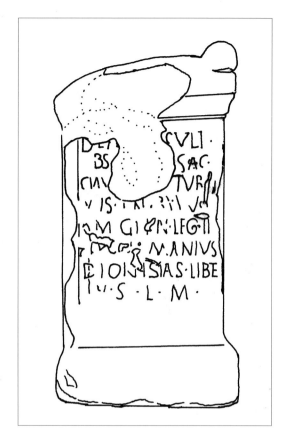

Fig. 24. This altar, found in 1790 on Stall Street on the site of the Pump Room, is one of two dedications made to Sulis for the safety and welfare of Marcus Aufidius Maximus, centurion of Legio VI Victrix, made on his behalf by two of his freedmen. The full restored text of this one reads *Deae Suli pro salute et incolumitate Marci Aufidi Maximi centurionis legionis VI Victricis Aufidius Eutuches lebertus votum solvit libens merito*. 'To the goddess Sulis for the welfare and safety of Marcus Aufidius Maximus centurion of Legio VI Victrix, Aufidius Eutuches his freedman, willingly and deservedly fulfilled his vow.' Either Eutuches or the stone-carver was responsible for *lebertus* instead of *libertus*. (*RIB* I 143)

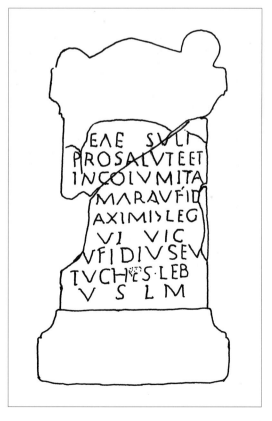

Fig. 25. An altar found in 1792 on the Pump Room site, most likely set up at the same time as *RIB* I 143, by another freedman of Marcus Aufidius Maximus. *Deae Suli pro salute et incolumitate Marci Aufidi Maximi centurionis legionis VI Victricis Marcus Aufidius Lemnus libertus votum solvit libens merito.* 'To the goddess Sulis for the welfare and safety of Marcus Aufidius Maximus centurion of Legio VI Victrix, Marcus Aufidius Lemnus his freedman, willingly and deservedly fulfilled his vow.' Perhaps the centurion Aufidius Maximus had gone to Aquae Sulis for a cure at the scared spring and the temple, and the vows made by his two freedmen were to offer an altar to Sulis, either in anticipation of a successful outcome, or after a successful cure had been obtained. (*RIB* I 144)

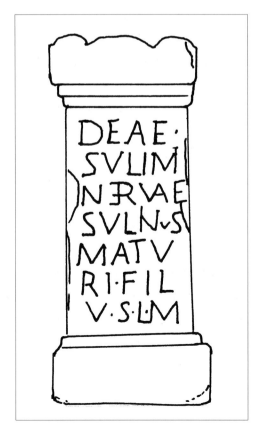

Fig. 26. This altar was found when the spring of the Hot Bath was being cleared out in 1774. *Deae Suli Minervae Sulinus Maturi filius votum solvit libens merito.* 'To the goddess Sulis Minerva Sulinus the son of Maturus willingly and deservedly fulfilled his vow.' Although the find spot is no indication of where the stone was set up, this altar may imply that Sulis Minerva could be worshipped at all the springs and baths. (*RIB* I 150)

Fig. 27. An altar found in the Cross Bath cistern in 1809. *Deae Suli Minervae et Numinibus Augustorum Gaius Curiatius Saturninus centurio legionis II Augustae pro se siusque votum solvit libens merito.* 'To the goddess Sulis Minerva and to the divine spirits of the Emperors Gaius Curiatius Saturninus centurion of Legio II Augusta for himself and his family willingly and deservedly fulfilled his vow.' The fact that two Emperors are involved in the dedication is indicated by the double-'G' in the abbreviation 'AUGG'. There were several occasions when two Emperors ruled together, so unless they are specifically named it can only be conjectured which Emperors are meant, but in this case they are thought to be Marcus Aurelius and Lucius Verus, which places the altar in the years AD 161–9. The phrase *pro se siusque* is an alternative version of *pro se et suis*, the suffix *-que* linking with the previous word, as in *Senatus Populusque*, Senate and People. Some of the letters on this inscription are ligatured, for instance in Curiatius, the letters 'T' and 'I' are joined, and in Saturninus the first 'N' is joined with the letter 'I'. The rightward-pointing arrow before the word 'LEG' is the symbol for centurion. (*RIB* I 146)

Fig. 28. A dedication stone, not an altar, found near the Great Bath around 1880. *Priscus Touti filius lapidarius cives Carnutenus Suli deae votum solvit libens merito.* 'Priscus son of Toutis, stonemason, tribesman of the Carnutes, to the goddess Sulis, willingly and deservedly fulfilled his vow.' Priscus came from Gaul, in the region of modern Chartres, where the capital of the Carnutes was situated. He may have worked on the buildings at Aquae Sulis, but there is no proof as to why he was there. The lettering is clear and ornate; perhaps he carved it himself? (*RIB* I 149)

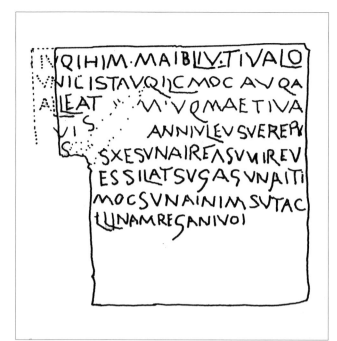

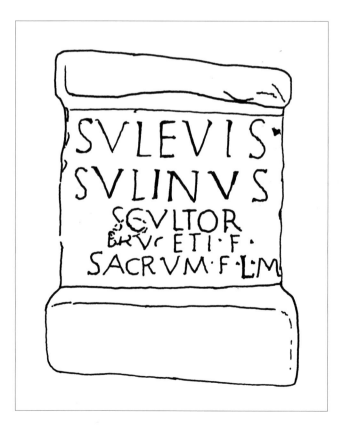

Above left: Fig. 29. Lead curse tablet found in 1880 in the reservoir of the sacred spring when the King's Bath had developed a leak and work was being done to try to stop it. The reservoir was unknown until that time, but was covered over again as soon as possible so the King's Bath could continue to function. *Qui mihi Vilbiam involavit sic liquat commodo aqua. Ella muta qui eam voravit si Velvinna Exsuperus Verianus Severinus Augustalis Comitianus Catusminianus Germanilla Jovina.* 'May whoever carried off Vilbia from me become as liquid as water. May whoever devoured her be struck dumb, whether Velvinna, Exsuperus, Verianus, Severinus, Augustalis, Comitianus, Catusminianus, Germanilla, or Jovina.' Plenty of suspects are listed here for Sulis to identify. The main problem is that no-one knows who or what Vilbia was. The usual interpretation is that someone has lost a girlfriend or a wife, but doubt has been cast on this idea. The word *voravit*, 'consumed', is slightly worrying. The words of the curse are written in the correct order but the letters of each word are written backwards, not uncommon on curse tablets. (*RIB* I 154)

Below left: Fig. 30. This inscription was found in lower Stall Street in 1753. It formed the base for a statue which is not known. *Sulevis Sulinus scultor Bruceti filius sacrum fecit libens merito.* 'To the Suleviae, Sulinus, a sculptor, son of Brucetus gladly and deservedly made this offering.' The same Sulinus, son of Brucetus, is known from an inscription at Cirencester, where his altar to the same goddesses, the Suleviae, was found with sculptures of the mother goddesses, which Sulinus may have produced himself or had made in his workshop. Like Priscus the stonemason (Fig. 28), Sulinus may have worked in Bath. (*RIB* I 151)

Right: Fig. 31. Found in the Hot Bath ruins in 1776, this stone may have been an altar or perhaps a statue base, but it was altered in the eighteenth century when someone smoothed the top and the sides. In the process, whoever it was perhaps removed the letters of the first line, which are assumed to have been 'DEA DIA', to match up with the 'NA' of the extant visible first line, thus reading to the goddess Diana. *Deae Dianae sacratissimae votum solvit Vettius Benignus, libertus.* 'To the most sacred goddess Diana, the freedman Vettius Benignus fulfilled his vow.' (*RIB* I 138)

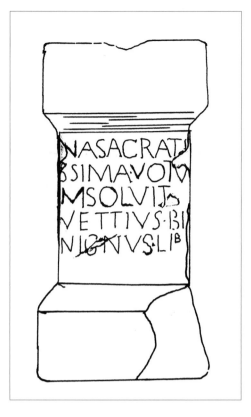

Below: Fig. 32. This stone is a building block, found in 1825 when the foundations were dug for the United Hospital, Lower Borough Walls. The text is only the lower part of a dedication, though to whom and why is not known. *Novanti filius pro se et suis ex visu possuit (sic).* '… son of Novantius set this up for himself and his family, from a vision.' The letters 'I' and 'T' of *posuit* are ligatured. (*RIB* I 153)

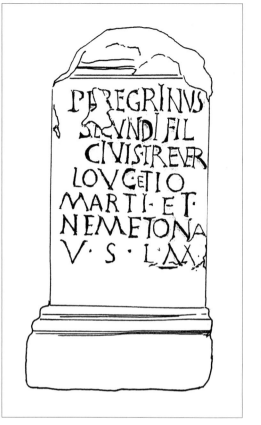

Fig. 33. Altar found in Stall Street in 1753. The top is broken off. *Peregrinus Secundi filius civis Trever Loucetio Marti et Nemetona votum solvit libens merito'*. Peregrinus son of Secundus, a citizen of the tribe of the Treveri, to Loucetius Mars and Nemetona, willingly and deservedly fulfilled his vow.' The goddess Nemetona ought to appear as Nemetonae in the dative case, since the dedication and vow had been made to her and Loucetius Mars. It has been argued that the stonemason made an error, presumably in not leaving enough room for an extra letter. Loucetius, or Leucetius Mars and Nemetona were worshipped in the Rhine area, sometimes separately and sometimes together. The goddess Sulis Minerva clearly tolerated the worship of other deities in the vicinity of her temple, so Peregrinus could bring his beliefs with him to Aquae Sulis. (*RIB* I 140)

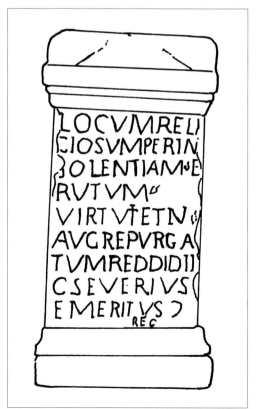

Fig. 34. This stone was found in lower Stall Street in 1753, not far from the statue base dedicated by Sulinus, son of Brucetus (fig. 30) and the altar of Peregrinus (fig. 33). *Locum religiosum per insolentiam erutum virtuti et numini Augusti repurgatum reddidit Gaius Severius Emeritus centurio regionarius.* 'This religious place was wrecked by insolence and newly cleansed has been restored to the virtue and deity of the Emperor, by Gaius Severius Emeritus, centurion in command of the region.' It is not stated in the inscription what had been destroyed, but contemporary locals and visitors would probably be perfectly aware of what had happened. The status of Severius Emeritus in Aquae Sulis is not clear. He may have been merely visiting and decided to restore the place out of his own pocket, to gain prestige, or he may have been the officer in charge of local government in the town. There are other examples of legionary centurions in charge of whole regions in the Empire, and two different centurions fulfilled the role at Ribchester in Lancashire. (*RIB* I 152)

Fig. 35. All the fragments shown here were found when the Pump Room was being rebuilt, but probably not all at the same time. The lettering of the various pieces is similar so they most likely belonged to the same inscription, thought to have belonged to the Façade of the Four Seasons. The restored Latin text, in which there are several gaps, would have read (fragments a, b and c) *Claudius Ligur … ae nimia vetustate … colegio longa seria annorum sua pecunia refici et repingi curavit.* 'Claudius Ligur … excessive age … the guild in long sequence of years … at his own cost had it repaired and repainted'. And fragment d, *Gaius Protacius … deae Sulis Minerva.* 'Gaius Protacius … of the goddess Sulis Minerva.' The inscription has many ligatured letters, some of which are conjoined with the following letter and carved in reverse, such as the letters 'E' and 'T' of *VETUS* in fragment a, and the 'E' and 'R' of *SERIA* in fragment c. There is not enough information to be able to say what exactly Claudius Ligur and Gaius Protacius had repaired, but it would most likely have been the Façade of the Four Seasons itself, or indeed the hypothetical building behind it. The text also proves that sculptures and lettering of inscriptions were brightly painted in Roman times. (*RIB* I 141)

Fig. 36. This tombstone was found in 1708 on the London Road at Walcot. Burials were forbidden inside the towns so the London Road and others out of Aquae Sulis would have been lined with tombstones. *Julius Vitalis fabriciensis legionis XX Valeriae Victricis stipendiorum IX annorum XXIX natione Belga ex collegio fabricensium elatus hic situs est.* 'Julius Vitalis, armourer of Legio XX Valeria Victrix served for nine years, lived for twenty-nine years, a tribesman of the Belgae, the funeral paid for by the Guild of armourers, lies here.' It has been suggested that Vitalis belonged to the Belgae of the *civitas Belgarum* at Winchester, and was therefore locally recruited into the legion. Examples of Britons in the Roman army are not unknown, but it did not become common until after the early second century, so it is perhaps more likely that Vitalis belonged to the Belgae of the Belgic parts of Gaul, Gallia Belgica, and was recruited there. (*RIB* I 156)

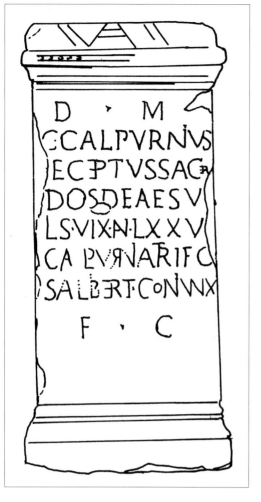

Fig. 37. This is a tombstone, shaped appropriately like an altar, for Gaius Calpurnius Receptus, the priest of Sulis Minerva. It was found in 1795 in Bathwick. *Dis Manibus Gaius Calpurnius Receptus sacerdos deae Sulis vixit annos LXXV Calpurnia Trifosa liberta coniunx faciendum curavit.* 'To the gods and shades Gaius Calpurnius Receptus priest of the goddess Sulis lived seventy-five years, Calpurnia Trifosa his freedwoman and wife set this up.' Receptus was presumably not the only priest of Sulis, but so far he is the only one for whom there is concrete evidence. The story behind the inscription tells how Receptus owned a slave called Trifosa and then freed her and married her, surely the basis for a novel. The ligatured lettering saves space on the stone, two of the most interesting examples being the insertion of a small reversed 'E' joined to the letter 'R', inserted into the 'C' of *sacerdos* in line three, and the abbreviated *annos* consisting of a letter 'N' with a cross-bar in the left-hand side, so it looks like 'AV' joined up. (*RIB* I 155)

Fig. 38. Tombstone found at East Hayes on the London Road in 1792. *Sergia tribu Antigonus Nicopoli emeritus ex legione XX annorum XLV hic situs est. Gavius Tiberinus heres faciendum curavit.* '… of the Sergian voting tribe, Antigonus from Nicopolis, *emeritus* from Legio XX, aged forty-five, lies here. His heir Gavius Tiberinus set this up.' Roman citizens were assigned to a voting tribe, even though, as the Empire expanded, many citizens probably never even saw Rome. Since the surviving top line is broken, the name Antigonus is restored from the lower fragment of the letter 'G' followed by 'ONUS'. It is a Greek name, appropriate for a man who came from Nicopolis in Epirus in Greece, whose Roman citizen inhabitants belonged to the Sergian voting tribe. The title *emeritus* is not part of Antigonus's name, but indicates that he had served his full term in the legion or possibly in more than one legion, and was now a veteran. (*RIB* I 160)

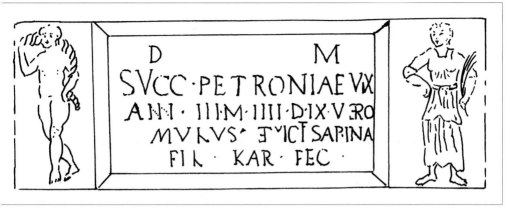

Fig. 39. This tombstone was built into the walls of the city near the North Gate. It was seen in 1600 but had been lost by the eighteenth century. Fortunately it was drawn before it disappeared. The figures flanking the inscription may not have originally belonged to it. *Dis Manibus Successae Petroniae vixit annos III menses III dies IX Vettius Romulus et Victoria Sabina filiae karissimae fecerunt.* 'To the gods and shades and to Successa Petronia, lived three years, three months and nine days. Vettius Romulus and Victoria Sabina set this up for the dearest daughter.' Many children must have died young in the Roman Empire, but not all of them had parents who went to the expense of setting up a tombstone. Perhaps the little girl had been brought to Aquae Sulis for a cure, which unfortunately failed. (*RIB* I 164)

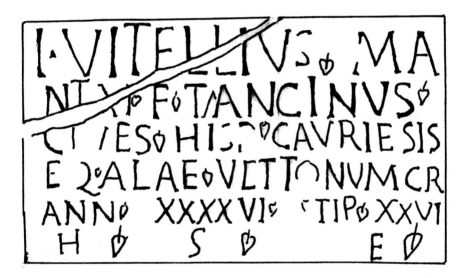

Fig. 40. This is the text of the broken tombstone for Lucius Vitellius Tancinus. The top half of the gravestone is missing, but enough of it survives to show the lower half of the cavalry horse and Tancinus's legs. It was found in 1736 in the old market place, near the modern Guildhall. *Lucius Vitellius Mantai filius Tancinus cives Hispanus Cauriensis eques alae Vettonum Civium Romanorum annorum XXXXVI stipendiorum XXVI hic situs est.* 'Lucius Vitellius Tancinus, son of Mantaius, tribesman of Caurium in Hispania, trooper of the *ala Vettonum*, Roman Citizens, aged forty-six, of twenty-six years' service, lies here.' Caurium was in the territory of the Vettones, in the Roman province of Hispania Lusitania, now modern Portugal. The tombstone may belong to the early period just after the conquest, in which case it is possible that Tancinus was stationed at the hypothetical fort at Bath. The *ala Vettonum* had at some stage earned prestigious battle honours, all the soldiers being granted Roman citizenship, a recognised award for auxiliary units whose soldiers had distinguished themselves in battle. Auxiliary soldiers normally had to complete twenty-five years of service to achieve citizenship. (*RIB* I 159)

Fig. 41. This tombstone was found in the later sixteenth century on the London Road, together with the tombstone of Gaius Murrius, described below. It is now lost, but the antiquarian John Horsley was able to make a drawing of it. *Dis Manibus Marcus Valerius Marci filius Latinus civis Equester miles legionis XX annorum XXXV stipendiorum XX his situs est.* 'To the gods and shades Marcus Valerius Latinus, son of Marcus, citizen of Equestris, soldier of Legio XX, aged thirty five with twenty years' service, lies here.' Equester refers to Noviodunum Colonia Julia Equestris, now modern Nyon. Valerius Latinus must have joined the legion at the age of fifteen, whereas the majority of the soldiers who died at Aquae Sulis had joined up at the age of about twenty. (*RIB* I 158)

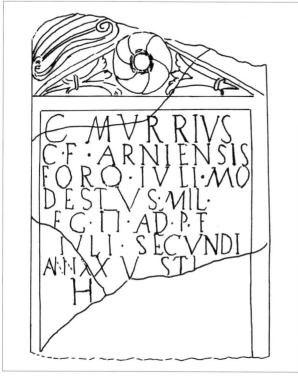

Fig. 42. This tombstone was found with that of Marcus Valerius Latinus (*RIB* I 158) in the later sixteenth century. The stone is no longer extant, but Horsley made a drawing of it. *Gaius Murrius Gai filius Arniensis Foro Julio Modestus miles legionis II Adiutricis Piae Fidelis centuria Iuli Secundi annorum XXV stipendiorum … his situs est.* 'Gaius Murrius Modestus, son of Gaius, of the Arniensian voting tribe, from Forum Julii, soldier of Legio II Adiutrix, from the century of Julius Secundus, aged twenty-five, of … years' service, lies here.' This tombstone may date from the period when Legio II Adiutrix was based at Chester, while Legio XX was probably in Scotland during and after the campaigns of Gnaeus Julius Agricola from around AD 78 to around AD 84. Forum Julii is now modern Frejus in France, and the note in *RIB* suggests that the Arniensian voting tribe is a spelling mistake for Aniensian. (*RIB* I 157)

Above left: Fig. 43. The antiquarian William Stukeley drew this tombstone inscription, which had been reused in the city wall between the North Gate and the West Gate. It is now lost. *Vibia Iucunda annorum XXX hic sepulta est*. 'Vibia Jucunda aged thirty lies buried here.' So far no-one has been rash enough to link Vibia Jucunda with Vilbia of the famous curse tablet (fig. 29). (*RIB* I 165)

Above right: Fig. 44. This stone formed the end of an actual tomb which has not survived intact. It was found in the walls near the North Gate in 1809. *Dis Manibus Mercatilla Magni liberta alumna vixit annum I menses VI dies XII*. 'To the gods and shades Mercatilla, freedwoman and foster daughter of Magnus, lived one year six months and twelve days.' The word *liberta* is more usually abbreviated to *lib* but is here represented by the single letter 'L'. (*RIB* I 162)

Centre: Fig. 45. Found in 1803 in the walls of the city, this tombstone is one of the few that have been found recording women in Aquae Sulis. *Rusoniae Aventinae civi Mediomatricae annorum LVIII hic sita est. Lucius Ulpius Sestius heres faciendum curavit*. 'To Rusonia Aventina citizen of the Mediomatrici tribe, aged fifty-eight, lies here. Her heir Lucius Ulpius Sestius set this up.' The *civitas* capital of the Mediomatrici was at modern Metz. (*RIB* I 163)

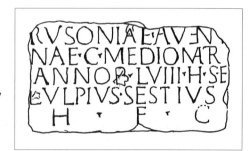

Below right: Fig. 46. This inscription was found in 1965 during excavations under the cellars of the Pump Room. *Deae Suli Lucius Marcius Memor, haruspex, donum dedit*. 'To the goddess Sulis, Lucius Marcius Memor, haruspex, gives this gift.' Lucius Marcius Memor may have trained as *haruspex* in another province before he arrived at Aquae Sulis. His occupation is not commonly attested in Roman Britain, so this may be the reason why the extra letters 'USP' were added to the otherwise centred 'HAR'. Marcius Memor may only have been visiting the healing centre, but it is more appealing to imagine that he had come to set up shop, as it were, working at the temple of Sulis Minerva in conjunction with the priests, examining the entrails and especially the livers of animals sacrificed on the altar in the temple precinct. The gift that Memor records may have been a statue of the goddess herself, but there is no evidence to support this.

a day, or even permanently watched, and the fires would have to be kept as far as possible at an even temperature. Leaks in the piping may have had to be mended and periodically the pipes and the drains may have had to be flushed out. The sacred spring would have to be cleaned of accumulated mud and sand. In the British climate, building maintenance would have been a perennial problem. If the baths at Aquae Sulis were run by a *conductor*, the person who took on the role would have to assess carefully whether the sum paid out initially could be recouped within the terms of the contract.

It is not known whether there was a fee for entry to the baths, but on analogy with what is known of other baths in the Roman Empire, there probably would have been a small charge, called *balneaticum*.[8] This term derives from *balnea*, meaning baths, but the larger establishments were more often called *thermae*. No ancient source explains what the precise difference in classification may have been. There are implications that *balneae* were perhaps smaller or inferior to *thermae*; perhaps *thermae* were of higher quality, or offered a greater number of services to customers. An inscription from Italy records the fact that the citizens of Lanuvium were building *thermae* to replace the *balneae*, which were very old and had gone out of use.[9] On occasions, wealthy patrons could pay the *conductor* directly for the entry fees for a whole day, or more than one day, sometimes for a whole year, especially if the person holding the purse strings was seeking election to some office.[10] For whatever period had been specified in the agreement between the benefactor and the *conductor*, all customers would be allowed in free of charge.

At Bath, there is no proof for any of this administrative detail, but an entry fee would contribute to the upkeep of the baths.

There were more facilities on offer at Aquae Sulis than there would have been in a conventional suite of public baths in other towns, because there were the additional healing elements of the spa and the religious aspects of the sacred spring, so perhaps the entry fees may have been more complicated than usual. The Romans were perfectly capable of operating a sort of docket system which allowed access to all the facilities or only part of them, much as in modern times it is usually possible to pay a reduced fee to visit the gardens of a stately home, but entry to the house as well as the gardens costs more. When the sacred spring was enclosed inside the rectangular vaulted building in the second century, access to it may have been restricted. Visitors could view it from a corridor off the Great Bath and may have had to pay extra to approach it from the temple precinct. Alternatively, perhaps only qualified religious personnel could access the spring once it was enclosed, to interact with the goddess on behalf of suppliants.

It is possible, but not certain, that the temple of Sulis Minerva and the baths would be administered and operated together as a single entity. Not all of the examples of inscribed stones and sculptures that have been found were necessarily from the temple precinct. Some were found in the baths, so it is at least a possibility that there was some kind of joint administration for this sort of thing, shared between the temple and the baths. While much of the decoration of the temple and the baths would be commissioned on a corporate basis, private individuals also desired to set up inscriptions and sculptures, to record their gratitude to the goddess or to fulfil their civic obligations, or just to show off their wealth and standing in the community. The numbers of inscribed altars and statues that have been discovered in the last three or four centuries probably represent only a small percentage of the dedications that were made by various people to Sulis and to other gods and goddesses.

It is probably safe to assume that a carved stone altar could not simply be put in place wherever the person dedicating it chose to install it. More likely some member of staff at the temple or the baths had to be consulted, and there would probably have been a process for allocating sites for the new stones to be set up. Similarly, anyone wanting to dedicate a statue could not simply commission it, bring it to the temple precinct, then put it down and leave it there without first negotiating with someone about its position and probably even its dimensions. Perhaps fees were paid as well, possibly in the form of hefty donations.

Builders and Artisans

When the baths and the temple of Sulis Minerva were being built at Bath, and when the alterations and rebuilding work was carried out at various stages in the second century, it would have been a good time to be a stonemason or a sculptor. It used to be thought that any Romano-British buildings of sophistication or grandeur must have been built by, or with the assistance of, legionary soldiers, because the legions comprised not just soldiers but also trained specialists in building, stone-carving, carpentry, metalwork, and so on. The presence of such specialists within a legion is documented by a second-century list of *immunes*, men who were responsible for a variety of tasks and who were excused the normal fatigues that other soldiers endured. There are also documented cases where military engineers were called in to finish off construction work when the locals got themselves into trouble. In a famous incident in North Africa, recorded on an inscription,[11] the citizens of Saldae in Mauretania Caesariensis tried to construct a tunnel to bring water to their town, but it all went wrong and they had to call in Nonius Datus, a veteran engineer of Legio III Augusta, to put it right.

Although Tacitus records that the governor of Britain, Gnaeus Julius Agricola, encouraged the Britons to build marketplaces, baths, forums and basilicas,[12] it should not be assumed that the soldiers built everything of note in the Romano-British towns. When the religious centre and bathing complex of Aquae Sulis were first established, and lots of other building work was going on in southern Britain, most of the soldiers were engaged in new conquests in northern England, Wales, and Scotland, so it is doubtful whether the governors of Britain during the reigns of Vespasian, Titus and Domitian would have been able to spare military specialists to help plan and build the temple and baths, at least in the summer campaigning seasons. Even if the soldiers returned to their bases in the winters between the campaigns, it would probably have been inadvisable to conduct building operations then. Nevertheless, it should be noted that some scholars are of the opinion that the Roman army did take an interest in developing spa towns in different parts of the Empire, so on this analogy it is possible that there was a military influence in the first phases of the foundation of Aquae Sulis.[13]

The question remains – who did do the building work? Some of the workmen who did the basic tasks may have been slaves, co-ordinated by Roman or Romanised building contractors, but for the finer embellishments the original craftsmen may have been brought in from Gaul. This conclusion is based on stylistic grounds, because the sculptural remains display some affinities with Gallic work. There is some support for the theory in that a dedication to Sulis was set up by Priscus, son of Toutis, in fulfilment of a vow. He describes himself as a *lapidarius*, or stonemason, and specifically states that he was a citizen of the Carnutes, whose tribal capital was at Chartres.[14] Priscus could have been a visitor seeking a cure at the spa or some other favour which was granted by Sulis. But he could also have been working on the construction or reconstruction of the baths, where the inscription was found, or on the temple and its precinct. There is nothing to date the stone, so there is no way of assigning Priscus to the original foundation of Bath, to the second-century alterations, or any developments that took place at a later time.

Apart from the existence of the several carved stones that must have been designed and made by someone, the only evidence for a sculptor at Bath is one inscription naming Sulinus, son of Brucetus,[15] who calls himself *scultor* (*sic*) on the altar that he dedicated to the Suleviae, the mother goddesses. He may have dedicated the altar in gratitude for some favour that had been granted, though he does not use the normal 'V.S.L.M.' formula. Sulinus dedicated another altar to the Suleviae at Cirencester,[16] and on this one he placed the usual formula at the end of the inscription. Although he does not call himself a sculptor at Cirencester, the altar was found together with a few sculptured stones, two of which depict the mother goddesses, so it is possible that he had produced these works himself and that his main depot was based at Cirencester. Whether or not he worked at Bath is unknown, but there would probably have been plenty of commissions there, if not from corporate sources in decorating the temple and the baths, then from private individuals who wished to decorate their homes, or dedicate statues, or perhaps have tombstones carved for their relatives.

During the original building and the later alterations, there would have been a need for many specialists who have left no trace of their names. There would have been several stonemasons, brick and tile manufacturers, bricklayers and carpenters to make the scaffolding for the erection of the buildings, and the wooden centring to support masonry or brick arches. There would have to be someone to mix the cement to the right consistency and correct quantities for the day's work, especially when the sacred pool was to be sealed, and again when the first phases of alterations were going on, especially when the massive vaulted roofs were built. For the first phase of the baths, workers would be required to line the pool and the Great Bath with thick sheets of lead, and to manufacture quantities of lead piping. There ought not to have been any problem at Bath in obtaining supplies of lead from nearby Charterhouse, nor should there have been any difficulty in obtaining the services of people who knew how to work it and what to do with it. All the multiple tasks associated with building work required someone who knew what they were doing, to supervise and keep a check on progress and quality, even if gangs of slaves did the actual hard graft.

There is evidence from within Bath itself for some industrial processes. There are traces of lead working and pewter manufacture, and of iron working in the so-called Citizen House, and of a smithy on the site of Bellott's Hospital.[17] These workshops may not be contemporary with the different phases of building work, but their existence serves to demonstrate that the people of Aquae Sulis organised and financed such industrial operations.

For the construction of the baths, copper and bronze workers would have been necessary to make the cauldrons and tanks for the hot water systems. Specialists would be called upon to install the furnaces and tanks, perhaps consulting the architectural manual written in the first century BC by Marcus Vitruvius Pollio. In this work, in book five, chapter ten, builders would be instructed how to arrange the tanks containing the cold, tepid and hot water, and how to build the suspended floors and hollow walls with box tiles to conduct the heat, all with economy of fuel-use in mind. Vitruvius also advises the designers of the baths to light them from the south, and to relate the size of the baths to the numbers of people who would use them. If the builders of the baths at Aquae Sulis had never heard of Vitruvius, they produced something for which he would probably have given wholehearted approval.

In addition to natural light admitted through the windows, artificial lighting for the baths would have required vast quantities of oil if they were to remain open into the dusk or even late at night in the dark. There is evidence that baths in some of the provincial cities stayed open after dark, if enough customers wanted to use them, and most especially where invalids and women bathed first, leaving the later hours for men.[18] Lamps were found in the baths at Pompeii, indicating that someone was there after dark, even it was only the caretaker.[19] In the British winter, the hours of daylight are so short that it seems likely that the temple precincts and the baths would remain open for a while after sunset, and if it is considered that oil lamps would not provide sufficient lighting to allow customers to use the baths of Roman Bath after dark, perhaps it is only a question of what people were accustomed to in the way of lighting. After all, in a much later age, the soirées in the assembly rooms of Bath went on far into the night, with a lighting system not much more sophisticated than a multiplicity of Roman oil lamps, and the Romans themselves attended dinner parties at night. When leaving their hosts they were accompanied through the dark streets to their homes by their slaves carrying torches or lamps. In a society that had never known street lamps and fluorescent lighting, oil lamps and torches would probably have been quite adequate.

For the other buildings at Aquae Sulis, there would have been plenty of employment opportunities. The restricted possibilities for excavations in modern Bath allow only a few glimpses here and there of workshops, houses, and buildings that may well have been accommodation for visitors. There are large areas of Bath that remain unexcavated, and it is more than probable that many more such buildings lie undetected under the modern streets. In all these buildings, not only construction workers and roof-tilers would have been needed, but also carpenters, plasterers, painters and decorators would have been employed. For the finer houses and business premises, mosaic manufacturers would have been called in, possibly with pattern books to agree on styles, to measure up rooms and estimate the expense. There were flourishing mosaic production firms in Cirencester, with distinctive styles of artistic layout and workmanship that can be easily identified. Aquae Sulis was smaller than other Romano-British towns, and it is possible that there were parts of it that remained empty of buildings, but there is no reason to suppose that the buildings that were erected were any less sophisticated than those of other settlements.

Bath Society

There is no doubt that many people of Roman Bath remain anonymous. With more excavations some of these anonymous people may be revealed, since it cannot be assumed that every single inscription that was ever produced has now been discovered. The great majority of the population will never be known, because they would not have been able to afford to dedicate altars or commission fine tombstones.

However, it is clear, even from the limited epigraphic evidence for the people of Aquae Sulis, that it was a culturally mixed society. At the upper level there are Roman citizens, and at the lower end freedmen, freedwomen, and slaves are attested, with several grades of people in between. The inhabitants and visitors were also ethnically diverse, coming from several provinces of the Roman Empire.

Slaves, as opposed to freedmen, are not so far represented in the epigraphic record, but a few of them have been recorded on curse tablets. Apart from the fact that they were called Lavidendus and Mattonius, and that Cunitius was married to Senovara, nothing else is known about them.[20]

For the freedmen who are attested, there is little more information about them than there is for these slaves. Vettius Benignus, *libertus*, fulfilled his vow by commissioning an altar to Diana at the Hot Bath.[21] More intriguing are the two separate altars dedicated to Sulis by two freedmen, Aufidius Eutuches[22] and Marcus Aufidius Lemnus,[23] for the health and welfare of their former master, Marcus Aufidius Maximus, centurion of Legio VI Victrix. This legion arrived in Britain with the Emperor Hadrian around AD 122, so the altars must date from some time after this. The circumstances behind these two dedications can only be guessed. Eutuches and Lemnus may have asked the goddess to help them gain their freedom, and made a vow that they would each dedicate an altar to her if their request was granted. But their altars were dedicated to Sulis for the health and welfare of the centurion Aufidius Maximus, which may involve more than simple gratitude to him for the reward of freedom. Did the centurion come to Aquae Sulis in the hope of a cure for some illness, or for a wound? Did Eutuches and Lemnus accompany him to the healing centre, each making a vow that they would dedicate an altar to Sulis if Maximus was restored to health? The fact that the vows were made and then fulfilled could indicate that on this occasion Sulis Minerva obliged, and Maximus was saved.

The ordinary people of Aquae Sulis appear more often on the curse tablets than on the inscriptions. The forms of personal names on the tablets reveals that the people of Aquae Sulis were a blend of Roman and Celtic stock, with a preponderance of the latter. They have left a record of their names, sometimes their status, and the crimes that had been committed against them, but there is nothing to reveal what they did for a living, or where they lived. Some of them may have come from the smaller settlements outside the town or from rural areas even further out. A man called Civilis lost a ploughshare and asked the goddess for help in retrieving it. Since it is unlikely that he brought the item into town and lost it there, he must have come into the town especially for the purpose of depositing a *defixio*.[24] Some of the people who left curse tablets in the sacred spring may have been free labourers working for someone, or residents who were running their own businesses in the town. One or two of them may have earned a living by accommodating the visitors.

The curse tablets record people from all levels of society, and both genders, but the predominant epigraphic record concerns men. Only a few women are attested. Claudia Trifosa, the freedwoman and then wife of the *sacerdos* Receptus, set up his tombstone when he died at age seventy-five.[25] Rusonia Aventina was a tribeswoman of the Mediomatrici, whose centre was at Metz.[26] The circumstances that brought her to Aquae Sulis are not known. Perhaps she had come seeking a cure, but she died at Bath aged fifty-eight, having appointed Lucius Ulpius Sestius her heir, who set up her tombstone. A lady called Vibia Jucunda died aged thirty, but there are no other details and her tombstone is now lost.[27]

The two most heart-rending tombstones record two infant girls. Successa Petronia died aged three years, four months and nine days, and was commemorated on her tomb by her parents Vettius Romulus and Victoria Sabina.[28] Perhaps she had been brought to the healing centre in the hope that Sulis Minerva could help. A child called Mercatilla died at just over eighteen months old. According to the interpretation of the wording on her gravestone, Mercatilla must have been born a slave, but was freed by a man called Magnius, who made her his foster-daughter.[29] Child mortality was fairly high in the Roman Empire, and tombstones assiduously recording the number of years, months, and days that they had lived are not uncommon.

Several people who are recorded at Bath originally hailed from other Roman provinces. Priscus the stonemason was a Gaul, a native of Chartres, and Peregrinus, who set up an altar to Loucetius Mars and Nemetona was from Trier. Rusonia Aventina, mentioned above, came from Metz. Among the soldiers who died at Bath, one whose name has not survived was a veteran of Legio

XX, originally from Nicopolis in Greece.[30] Two other legionaries of Legio XX came from Gaul. Marcus Valerius Latinus,[31] who joined the army aged fifteen and served for twenty years, was a native of Colonia Julia Equestris (modern Nyon). Julius Vitalis served as an armourer in the legion, and when he died after serving for nine years, aged only twenty-nine, his colleagues from the Guild of Armourers paid for his tombstone.[32] The inscription describes him as *natione Belga* which could possibly indicate that he was a native of the newly created British tribe of the Belgae, whose *civitas* capital was at Winchester. But it is generally considered that he could not be a British native, because the tombstone belongs stylistically to the late first or early second century, and it is thought that local recruitment of Britons into the legions would not have begun so early. Legionaries were supposed to be Roman citizens, as opposed to auxiliary soldiers who were non-citizens, but these soldiers earned citizenship after twenty-five years' unblemished service. If there was a shortage of manpower or an emergency, it was not unknown for the military authorities to employ legal fictions to convert non-Romans with native names to Roman citizens with Roman names, no questions asked, which is just possibly what happened to Julius Vitalis, but it is considered more likely that Vitalis was originally from the province of Gallia Belgica. Another Gaul, Gaius Murrius Modestus, from Forum Julii (modern Frejus), served in Legio II Adiutrix, and died aged twenty-five.[33] He would probably have moved with the legion from its base at Lincoln to the fortress at Chester, at around the time that the temple and baths were being built at Aquae Sulis.

The existence of the baths and the temple of Sulis Minerva would very rapidly attract a wide variety of people intent on making money. Visitors would have to be accommodated, probably for long periods while they underwent a course of treatment. Around them would gather vendors of food and drink, reputable doctors and dubious quacks, eye specialists, masseurs, hairdressers, prostitutes and pimps, trinket and souvenir sellers, purveyors of lead sheets to write curses on, and legal advisers to help with composing them. Ultimately, for everyone, visitors and residents alike, there would be a need for someone to carve a nice tombstone for those who could afford them. Plenty of work, then, and opportunities for enrichment, at Aquae Sulis.

All this cacophony of people is inferred rather than attested, though daily life at Aquae Sulis is probably appositely summarised in the frequently quoted passage of Seneca,[34] who described to a friend what it was like to live in an apartment over a suite of public baths in Rome, where people doing their exercises grunted and wheezed, the masseurs slapped and pummelled their clients or rather their victims, the hair-pluckers removed hairs from people's armpits with accompanying shrieks, and people outside added to the yelling to advertise their wares. The fact that Bath was supposed to be a healing centre would not necessarily guarantee peace and quiet.

Outside the Town

The line of the walls of Bath may have been marked out in the second century by an earthen bank and ditch. There would have been nothing primitive about the first walls, since the defences of several Roman towns started life in the same way. Probably in the fourth century, the earth ramparts were replaced in stone. The polygonal walls enclose a relatively small area compared to other Romano-British towns, the central feature being the temple and baths, taking up a large percentage of the space within the walls.

It should not be imagined that the walls marked a sharp division between settled town and unsettled countryside. Smaller settlements in the immediate vicinity of Bath have been identified to the north of the town on the west side of the River Avon, and across the river at Bathwick, where an early Roman fort may have been situated. North-west of Bath, groups of burials have been found, which may indicate the presence of villages nearby, and to the south between the town and the River Avon, near the ford at Cleveland Bridge, excavations have shown that there was a collection of buildings, interpreted as houses, shops and workshops.[35]

The land around Bath is fertile, the main agricultural produce of the region in Roman times being grain and wool, and livestock would have consisted of sheep and cattle, which could provide meat, milk and cheese and also hides. Clustered in groups to the north-west and south-east of the town, considerable numbers of local villas were established, most of them probably working farms rather than palatial dwellings, though even the rich villa owners would have farmed the land on their estates, employing stewards and numbers of slaves. Agriculture was the foremost generator of income in the Roman world. A glance at the last two editions of the Ordnance Survey maps of Roman Britain shows that similar clusters existed around Ilchester, Cirencester and Winchester. Such a concentration of villa sites indicates that the land was worth farming, but the maps can be deceptive, because the villas may have been built and occupied successively rather than contemporaneously. The highest concentration probably did not begin until the third century, and the apogee of villa society came in the fourth century, when very much more elaborate villas were built.

Supplying the Town

The resident population and the visitors to Aquae Sulis would obviously require provisions of food and household goods, and when the alterations to the baths and the temple were undertaken, the workforce was probably recruited from other areas, and would temporarily increase the numbers of people in the town needing to be housed and fed. There is no definite evidence for shops in Aquae Sulis, but it is difficult to imagine that there were none. A building of the later third century, in the vicinity of the modern Visitor Centre for the abbey, has been tentatively identified as a shop, but with no evidence of what might have been sold there.[36]

When the temple and baths were built at Aquae Sulis, and people began to settle there and visitor numbers grew, there would be a ready market for the producers of the grain and wool that were the staples of the region. People had to eat and clothe themselves, the latter being of prime importance at Bath, given the alarming rate of thefts of cloaks, gloves and other items of clothing. There is little solid evidence to illustrate the commerce of the town, except that there was an excellent road system into and out of Bath, leading to and from other towns, so produce could be brought in easily enough. Much depends on how goods for sale were brought to the town, in wagon loads from a villa or group of villas after harvest, accompanied by teams of people to accompany the produce, with the aim of selling all of it at once, or whether goods arrived in small amounts on a regular basis, carried by private sellers. In the medieval era, the statutory distance between markets was 6 miles. This figure was calculated according to how far traders could be expected to walk, set up their stalls, remain at the market to sell their produce, and then walk home, all within one day. Small traders from the immediate surroundings of Aquae Sulis could have provided milk, cheese and eggs and home-manufactured goods such as small amounts of home-woven textiles or ready-made clothing. No-one can say that this is how it worked.

The bulk of the food supply surely came from the villas, but it is not really known how the villas contributed to the economy of Aquae Sulis, or any other town. Many of the villas were situated within a radius of 25 kilometres of Bath. The distances were not impossible for transport, but would probably have been more difficult in winter. The owners of villas, whether they were very rich or only moderately wealthy, would need a market for their surplus production to bring in cash with which to buy goods such as furniture, tools and kitchen equipment that they could not necessarily produce for themselves at home. It is not known how the supply of food would have been organised. Perhaps some farmers were under contract, or entered into an agreement each year according to what they were planting and the likely yields. After the harvest of grain and other crops, there would be the problem of storage. Was there a granary in the town? Was grain stock bought corporately and then guarded and regularly distributed, or was it all left to private enterprise?

Inside the town, there would surely have been bakers' shops, butchers and livestock sellers, shops for household goods such as pots and pans, knives and metal implements, and textiles such as cushions and curtains and bolts of cloth, all of which are attested and illustrated in tremendous detail on relief sculptures in other parts of the Roman Empire, notably Trier. Most of these postulated shopkeepers would buy their goods from the surrounding area and further afield, from specialist manufacturers.

No site has yet been identified as a marketplace, or *macellum*, as there was at Cirencester, but there may still have been regulated market days at Aquae Sulis, possibly with different areas for the sale of grain and bread, meat, fruit and vegetables, none of which implied activity necessarily required a designated market hall or even any building at all, so there may be nothing to find by excavation except an open space where stalls may have been set up. This speculation borders on the realms of near-fantasy, for which there is no archaeological evidence. When examining how Roman towns were provisioned, it is easy to forget, in the age of enormous supermarkets where strawberries can be bought in February, how the supply of food was once strictly regulated by the seasons, and how much more limited and fragile the Roman food economy would have been before the introduction of modern staples like potatoes and rice, and the invention of domestic freezers.

With a ready-made tourist industry, other vendors selling non-essential items would have been attracted to the town. It is likely that people came to sell souvenirs, jewellery, and items suitable for offerings to the goddess Sulis. Exploitation of an assemblage of people with money to spend, all gathered on one place for a while, and relatively vulnerable if they had come to find relief for illnesses, is not a modern phenomenon.

How Local was Local Government?

The status of the settlement at Aquae Sulis is not known.[37] For the sake of simplicity it is easier to call it a town, but there is no information to help with its classification. It does not fit into any of the known categories of cities and towns, ranging from the most prestigious *coloniae* to the smallest village, or *vicus*. It was not a *civitas* capital, and as already mentioned in a previous chapter, according to the geographer Ptolemy, writing in the second century AD, Aquae Sulis was assigned to the *civitas* capital of the Belgae, Venta Belgarum, modern Winchester, as one of its towns. It has been pointed out by more than one author that the distance between Bath and Winchester is impossibly long, over 80 kilometres, which would make it difficult for local government to be carried out effectively. Communications between Winchester and Bath would have been slow. Using relays of horses, a rider could cover the distance in a day, but that would probably only happen in exceptional circumstances. It is assumed that, because of the relative isolation of Bath, some kind of administrative centre must also have existed in the town.[38]

The problem is that no buildings have yet been identified that could have served as such an administrative centre. It is generally agreed that the prime indicator that a town was self-governing is the presence of a forum and basilica. Although a forum is sometimes labelled the marketplace, this is misleading. A true market, where produce was sold, was usually called a *macellum*. The forum was the place where administrative functions were carried out and probably records were kept, and the basilica was the legal centre where the judicial courts were housed. Nothing that could be labelled as a forum has been found at Bath, but there are large areas that have not been excavated, so it remains a possibility that one day discoveries will be made that overturn this negative statement.

The foundations for some large building or precinct that were discovered to the east of the temple probably formed part of another temple precinct on the same alignment as that of the temple of Sulis Minerva, but these foundations may possibly have belonged to a forum. Although the remains of the postulated *tholos* temple, attested by fragments of its stonework, are thought to lie underneath the west end of the abbey, if there ever was a forum at all in Bath, aligned west to east perhaps, like the temple of Sulis Minerva and its precinct, then underneath the abbey is as good a place as any, reminiscent of the Minster at York, founded on the remains of the legionary headquarters building but aligned at an angle to the Roman building. If the postulated forum was indeed at this location, it would have formed a central unit with the temple of Sulis and the baths, and there would have been direct access, via what is now High Street, to and from the north gate. The problem is that it is not absolutely certain if the medieval walls of Bath and the layout of the principal roads still reflect the Roman town plan, so the course of High Street and the exact site of the north gate may not have been relevant in the Roman period. A number of Roman tombstones were found in the walls of this gate. They would originally have stood outside the town along the approach road, but it is not possible to say whether they were incorporated into the defences by the Roman or the medieval inhabitants, or to state categorically that the Roman road came into the town at this point. But it probably did, and a forum situated directly in line with it is not out of the question.

Some authors have insisted that Aquae Sulis was primarily a religious centre, implying that it existed without any form of town government of its own. It is true that there is no evidence for administrative buildings, and perhaps more to the point there is no trace whatsoever for town councillors at Bath. The members of the town council are among the most likely people to have left a record of themselves and their achievements, making sure that their names were mentioned and their dignified rank was recorded, but nothing has been found to attest any member of the government of Aquae Sulis. The only recorded decurion had nothing to do with government in the town. He was an eighty-year-old man who died there. His name has not survived, but he is recorded as a decurion from Glevum, modern Gloucester.[39] Perhaps the decurions of Venta Belgarum appointed local dignitaries as their representatives or deputies at Aquae Sulis, but there is no concrete evidence that they did so, and if this was how government was carried out, it would mean that every little detail would have to be constantly referred back to the town council at Winchester. It could be the case that representatives were sent at regular intervals to discuss business, to oversee judicial cases, and most especially to collect taxes. The decurions of the *ordo* were responsible for gathering their own local taxes and also the provincial taxes as laid down by the Imperial procurator, and it is unrealistic to imagine that Aquae Sulis escaped the fiscal networks of the province.

However Aquae Sulis was governed, there would have been a need for a rudimentary administrative system, to keep the streets clean, to maintain law and order, administer justice, regulate the markets and oversee building work so that no-one encroached on the streets or impinged on anyone else. When the earth defences were first built in the second century, permission would have to be sought from the provincial governor and through him from the Emperor. It was not simply a matter of a local council deciding on the spur of the moment that a circuit of walls would be a good thing and a nice status symbol, because fortifications could be used to defy the government and therefore had to be officially sanctioned. The fact that earthen ramparts, succeeded by stone walls, were built at Bath indicates that someone was in charge of organising the scheme, going through the proper channels to the governor, and then carrying out the work. It would seem to be slightly cumbersome to do all this through a town council situated 80 kilometres away.

There are, however, slight hints that certain persons wielded some influence in the town, if not formal administrative authority. Fragments of a long inscription from the so-called Four Seasons façade were found in 1790 recording two names, Claudius Ligur and Gaius Protacius.[40] The fragmented inscription reveals that Claudius had repaired and redecorated a building that had suffered over the years, presumably the façade of the Four Seasons itself, and Gaius Protacius made a dedication to Sulis. There is no slot in the extant wording for any title that might suggest that these men with Roman names were members of the town council. They may have simply been wealthy citizens of Aquae Sulis, who devoted time and money to the repair of buildings in order to enhance their own standing in the town. This was a normal procedure in Roman society. Rich men were expected to contribute to their communities by erecting buildings, and providing amenities and works of art, as well as paying their taxes.

A more definite hint of some form of local government derives from an altar found in the lower part of Stall Street in 1753, and now in the Roman Baths Museum.[41] It records the destruction of some unknown monument and its repair by Gaius Severius Emeritus, who describes himself as centurion in charge of the region. This is indicated at the bottom of the inscription, by means of a transposed letter 'c' facing the wrong way, a common economical method of signifying the rank of centurion, sometimes rendered as a 'v' on its side with the sharp end pointing to the right. The reverse 'c' is followed by the abbreviation 'REG ...', which is squeezed in at the base of the inscription, as though it was an afterthought, but is clear enough that the abbreviations should be read as *centurio regionis*, or *regionarius*.

Local government by a legionary centurion was a useful method of controlling an area, especially where there were no civilian towns in the immediate vicinity, but it is more common in the militarised areas. In Britain, perhaps the most famous examples derive from the fort at Ribchester in Lancashire, where two inscriptions were set up in the third century recording legionary centurions in command of the unit stationed at the fort, with additional authority over the area as well. Probably around AD 225 to 235, Titus Floridius Natalis, centurion of an unnamed legion, rebuilt a temple at Ribchester at his own expense.[42] He describes himself as *praepositus numeri et regionis*, officer in command of the military unit at Ribchester, which he does not name, and also the area. The title *praepositus* usually referred to an officer who had been placed in a temporary command, and the title had no connotations of rank, so not all *praepositi* would be centurions. A few years after Natalis had rebuilt the temple, another commander had been appointed. Aelius Antoninus, centurion of Legio VI Victrix, made a dedication to the god Apollo Maponus, for the welfare of the Emperor.[43] The stone probably served as the base of a statue. Like Natalis, Antoninus was seconded from his legion to command the Ribchester unit, which is named this time as the Sarmatian cavalry, and he also describes himself as *praepositus regionis*.

A single inscription from Bath naming a centurion in command of the region is not enough to construct a complete system of local government. Emeritus may have been at Bath coincidentally with other duties. It is suggested that he may have been chiefly concerned with the administration of an Imperial estate, where lands belonged to the Emperor, so he may have merely been a visitor to Aquae Sulis. The inscription records that something, a monument or a building, had been destroyed at Bath and that Emeritus repaired it, so it could be that he had arrived there just as some destruction had taken place, and magnanimously decided to undertake repairs on behalf of the town.

On the other hand he may have been specially appointed to take control at Aquae Sulis. Since the region which Severius Emeritus commanded is not specifically identified, it presumably concerns the area around Bath, which lies in relative isolation, 80 kilometres from Winchester and around 50 kilometres from any other large town. The destruction of some unknown monument may indicate that there had been some unrest, and that Emeritus had been called in to restore order as well as buildings. Several scenarios are possible, but this inscription indicates that there was a legionary officer with authority, perhaps on a temporary basis, in the area around the town of Aquae Sulis. This does not necessarily preclude the existence of a town council at Bath. If there were such a body, the appointment of Emeritus could have been made to give him temporary authority while a crisis was dealt with, and the councillors would have been subordinate to him. People would probably tend to do as they were told by a legionary centurion.

Despite all the speculation and brave words, it has to be admitted that no-one knows how Aquae Sulis functioned, what its true status was or how it was governed within the province of Britain. Archaeological excavators of the future must surely pray to Sulis Minerva for the discovery of an inscription, however fragmentary, with just one tiny glimpse of a decurion of Aquae Sulis.

6

BATH DECLINES & REVIVES

The third century was not a happy time for the Roman Empire, but from the nadir of the AD 260s, when every frontier fell and the Empire temporarily fragmented, there was a recovery that averted the final disintegration for another 200 years. The first changes that would affect Roman Britain in the longer term began in the third century. From AD 208 to 211 the Emperor Severus and his sons Caracalla and Geta campaigned in northern Britain, subduing the tribes of Caledonia and reconstituting the frontier of Hadrian's Wall. Severus's repairs to the Wall were so extensive that in the nineteenth century archaeologists thought that he had been responsible for building the Wall, and the frontier that Hadrian established must have been the deep ditch to the south of the Wall, known since the days of the Venerable Bede as the Vallum. Then an inscription[1] was discovered naming Hadrian's provincial governor Aulus Platorius Nepos, so Hadrian was duly credited with the entire concept of a solid frontier, and also all of the building work.

Administratively the Severans made two changes to Britain. Either Severus or his son Caracalla divided the province into two smaller units, named Britannia Superior, governed by an ex-consular based in London, and Britannia Inferior, governed by an equestrian *praeses*, ranking below the senatorial class, based at

York. Aquae Sulis was in the Superior province. The titles Inferior and Superior have nothing to do with judgement of quality. Provinces labelled Superior were generally closer to Rome, and Inferior further away.

The other administrative change occurred in AD 212 or 213, when the Emperor Caracalla passed a law called the *Constitutio Antoniniana*, bestowing Roman citizenship on all free-born inhabitants of the Empire. According to customary usage, those who obtained citizenship from a Roman official took the family name of their benefactor. Caracalla is a nickname derived from the Gallic cloak that the Emperor habitually wore. His true name as a son of Lucius Septimius Severus was Septimius Bassianus, but his official Imperial name was Marcus Aurelius Antoninus, linking the Severans, who had obtained power at the point of the sword, to that of the Emperor Marcus Aurelius, who came to power more legitimately as the adoptive descendant of Hadrian. From the time of the *Constitutio* the name Aurelius proliferated all over the Empire. For the people of Aquae Sulis, judging from the surviving names on inscriptions and more usually on curse tablets, this edict made little difference, and Celtic names still predominated.

One of the unfortunate features of the third century, from the archaeologist's point of view, is the beginning of the decline of epigraphic evidence. People gradually stopped setting up inscriptions, so with the passage of time into the fourth century, there is less and less personal information about the inhabitants of Roman Britain. For the Empire in general the third century was chaotic and dangerous, most especially for people living within reach of the frontiers. Tribes outside the Empire began to penetrate Imperial territory, either for hit-and-run raids or sometimes demanding permission to settle because life inside the Empire seemed less threatening than life outside it.

People were displaced from the North Sea coasts of Germany and the Netherlands as sea levels rose and lands became infertile because of the salt content. There are signs of aggressive invasions of territory further north. The subsequent movement of tribes affected those nearer to the frontiers, and the Romans found themselves threatened along the Rhine and Danube, forced to mount defensive wars to contain the tribes. In AD 235 the Emperor Severus Alexander was with the army on the Rhine when he was assassinated by the troops, who declared for their general Maximinus Thrax, the Thracian. He was a member of the equestrian or middle class, the first non-senatorial Emperor and the first of the soldier-Emperors whose reigns spanned the next two and a half decades, while various generals fought each other while at the same time trying to fight frontier wars. The future of the Empire looked a little brighter with the accession of Valerian and his son Gallienus as co-Emperors. Gallienus could deal with the western provinces, while his father attended to the eastern frontier where the Parthian dynasty had been succeeded by the more aggressive Persians. In AD 260 it all went wrong. Valerian was captured by the Persians and his army was defeated. The Palmyrene nobleman Odenathus, and then his wife Zenobia, succeeded in keeping the eastern provinces together, protected from Persian attacks. The Emperor Gallienus was unable to come to their assistance, being fully preoccupied with the west, where the response to raids across the frontiers was the establishment of a separate Empire, the *Imperium Galliarum*, ruled by Emperors selected by the troops. The Empire was thus divided into three, with the central portion ruled by Gallienus, with limited resources to combat the tribes pouring across the Danube and the Alps, threatening Italy itself.

The two British provinces were not directly affected by the turmoil of the AD 260s, but there was a detectable material decline in living standards. As part of the Gallic Empire, life went on, but the first signs of trouble with sea-borne raiders had begun, making trading ventures across the North Sea less secure. When the Empire was reunited by the Emperor Aurelian in the AD 270s, things may have improved a little but shortly afterwards Britain was once again split off from the Empire under the general Marcus Aurelius Mausaeus Carausius. He had been appointed around AD 285 to command a fleet against the Saxon pirates in the Channel, based at Boulogne. The story goes that he was initially successful in defeating and capturing some of the pirates, but had not been quite so assiduous about returning the recaptured booty to its original owners, so he fled to Britain and proclaimed himself Emperor. He tried to reconcile his new regime with the legitimate Emperors Diocletian and Maximianus, but they refused to recognise him. When Carausius was assassinated by one of his own men, Allectus, the end came quickly. Constantius Caesar, also known as Constantius Chlorus, conquered the rebels and brought the British provinces back into the Empire. A medal was struck to commemorate the occasion, proclaiming modestly that Constantius had 'restored the eternal light' to the two provinces, which had probably not noticed that they had been in the dark.

By the early years of the fourth century, Britain had been divided into four smaller provinces. There were similar changes all over the Empire. Diocletian recognised that the Roman Empire, beset externally by tribesmen trying to get in, and internally by inflation and unrest, was too large for one man to rule, so he had created the Tetrarchy, with two senior Emperors – himself and Maximianus – with the title of Augusti, and two junior Emperors called Caesars, Constantius Chlorus in the west, and Galerius in the east. This division was intended to provide commanders and armies in four quarters of the Empire, to keep the peace and protect the frontiers, but it all failed eventually because the four Emperors fought each other as well as enemies of Rome.

The administrative changes started by Diocletian endured for longer. Diocletian divided up the provinces into smaller units, and then grouped them together into Dioceses, each placed under an official called a *vicarius*. The chain of command now descended from the Emperors via the Praetorian prefects whose military responsibilities had been devolved onto the generals, then via the *vicarii*, literally deputies of the prefects, to the governors of the provinces, with the title *praeses*. These were now usually non-military men, with responsibility for civilian affairs. The troops were commanded by a *Dux*, which literally means 'leader' and is the origin of Mussolini's title Duce. The *Dux* could be in command of the troops of one province, or sometimes of the armies of several provinces grouped together. In Britain, it had become necessary to defend not only the northern frontier, but also the coasts. The forts of the so-called Saxon Shore were eventually under a unified command, but had not started out as a single unified concept of coastal defence. The forts are of different ages, the first ones established in the third century, with more forts added as need arose, all ultimately brought together as though that had always been the intention.

The four British provinces were Maxima Caesariensis, most likely governed from London, Flavia Caesariensis, probably based on Lincoln, and Britannia Prima and Britannia Secunda. The latter province was most likely governed from York. Aquae Sulis was probably in Britannia Prima, with the headquarters at Cirencester, though this assumption derives from one inscription of the mid-fourth century, recording a man called Lucius Septimius as *primae* *provinciae rector.*² If Cirencester was the seat of government of Prima, then Aquae Sulis was closer to the centre of government than ever before and may have benefited from the association.

It may have been the Emperor Constantine who brought Diocletian's administrative changes to fruition. Constantine was the son of Constantius, and was in Britain on campaign with his father when Constantius died in AD 306. The troops immediately hailed him Emperor. It took him the best part of two decades to emerge as sole Emperor after defeating all his rivals. He tried to reconcile the religious differences that had sprung up over the Empire, issuing the Edict of Milan in AD 313 which was supposed to guarantee religious toleration across the Empire. Ultimately Constantine was responsible for the adoption of Christianity as the official state religion, and he abandoned Rome as the capital, founding another at Byzantium, renamed Constantinople. Rome had long since ceased to be the most important centre in any case. Emperors now needed to be with their armies, closer to the frontiers, and made their residences in other cities, such as Milan and Trier in the west. Constantinople was closer to the threatened areas of the Danube and the east, where the focus now lay.

The fourth century witnessed the zenith and the nadir of the fortunes of Roman Britain. In the south, there was an upsurge in the number of extremely well-appointed villas. These are not just self-sufficient farms. They positively ooze wealth and an appreciation of the finer things in life. It is suggested that there had been an influx of Gallic landowners in the fourth century, though it might be expected that such people would already have migrated during the turmoil of the AD 260s in Gaul. If not from Gaul, the villa owners may have been town councillors turning their backs on town life and the responsibilities, not to mention the drain on finances, which had become an increasingly burdensome part of local government.

While villas flourished as never before, the towns did not share in the prosperity of the fourth century. It had become too expensive to maintain one's position as a town councillor, and the prestige involved was not enough to tempt people to undertake their duties. Being appointed to the *ordo* was no longer an honour but a rapid road to bankruptcy. It was increasingly difficult to collect the taxes, and the councillors had to make up the shortfall. In some parts of the Empire the large landowners could become territorial magnates with the ability and resources to defy the tax collectors and the recruiting officers, keeping their labourers safe from the depredations of government officials. For Britain the evidence is contradictory. On the one hand there are the prosperous villas and on the other hand in the later fourth century there are parts of towns that have been abandoned and signs that cultivation of crops had taken over, or even been squashed into small areas between dwellings in the towns. And yet, in AD 359, the Emperor Julian restarted the lapsed shipments of grain from Britain to Germany,³ indicating that there was a surplus in production. No protests have been recorded from landowners, complaining that their very livelihoods were being purloined.

The Romano-Britons of the later fourth century were subject to a series of misfortunes. Raids on the coasts and sometimes far inland caused considerable distress, necessitating the presence of the western Emperor Constans in AD 343, though his campaigns are not elucidated. Ten years later the revolt by the *vicarius* Martinus was brutally suppressed by Paul Catena, the Chain, sent by the Emperor. In AD 360 the raids of the Picts and Scots across the northern frontier escalated, and in AD 367 attacks from all quarters by land and sea were labelled by the Romans as the *Conspiratio Barbarica* as though the Picts, Scots, Frankish and Saxon pirates had conspired together to attack Britain and northern Gaul. The Emperor's companion, *Comes* Theodosius, usually translated as Count, restored order, but it was short-lived. A series of attempts at usurpation plagued Britain and reduced its military strength. In the AD 380s, Magnus Maximus was declared Emperor in Britain, and probably took the majority of the troops with him to Gaul where he was defeated. More troops may have been removed by the general Stilicho, in defence of Gaul, around AD 400. In quick succession, three more usurpers called Marcus, Gratian, and Constantine III were raised as Emperors, and ended in disaster in Gaul, reducing the troops in Britain yet again. By AD 410 the British had divorced themselves from the rule of Constantine III and expelled all the Roman officials, and the western Emperor Honorius supposedly recalled the troops, though there is now some doubt about this once accepted fact. There were probably hardly any troops left in the island anyway.

Bath in the Later Roman Period

Until the fourth century the operators of the baths and the temple of Sulis Minerva tried to keep things running. Somebody thought it worthwhile to repave the temple precinct, which suggests continued usage, but whoever was in charge had no compunction about using pagan sculptures to do it. The Christians would not trouble themselves about devotional monuments to pagan gods and goddesses. For some time, pagan shrines such as Uley and Lydney in Gloucestershire, and indeed the temple of Sulis

Minerva, had continued in use, and Christians and pagans had managed to live side by side until the later fourth century. In AD 391 all forms of pagan worship were banned, so the temple of Sulis would be redundant. It had probably already gone out of use by then.

The baths too had probably been abandoned for several years. In the later phases of alterations there had been a reduction on the services offered.[4] At the western end of the baths the *caldarium* was converted into a cold bath in the shape of an elongated oval, and perhaps to compensate for the loss of the heated room, more heat had been directed to the *tepidarium*, though this would hardly be an exact substitute. The hot room, the *laconicum* was kept up and the associated warm bath was refitted. Another small bath was built to the south. It seems as though perhaps fewer people were using the baths, requiring smaller rooms. The eastern end of the baths required more labour. The hypocausts had been flooded from the River Avon, as a result of rising sea levels. To combat this, the Roman engineers had taken up all the floors and raised the level of the hypocausts themselves by inserting a layer of clay pressed between the supports, hopefully above the flood line. This is rather more laborious than having a new carpet fitted, and presumably there was enough demand for the services offered by the baths to justify the work and the operators of the baths thought it worthwhile to make the attempt to keep the place functioning despite the flooding. But it failed in the end.

Rising sea levels had begun in the third century, and could not be stopped at Bath. It might have been physically possible to deal with the floods by creating new drains and even raising the floors of the entire building, installing new piping to deliver waters of the hot springs at a higher level. The engineering skills may not have been entirely lost, but the will to put them into effect and the finance were lacking. The temple of Sulis Minerva may have been in decline for some time as the Christians gained in supremacy, and though the benefit of the curative waters of the spring could be shared by everyone no matter what their beliefs, the disturbed times and the rising river levels defeated any plans that might have been formed to save the baths. Ultimately they were abandoned. A small phrase, describing an enormous change.

Bath was not alone. The public baths at Wroxeter went out of use around AD 330 and those at Canterbury twenty years later. Around the same time the amphitheatres at London and Cirencester were abandoned, and at Verulamium no-one used the theatre after AD 375. The raids of the *Conspiratio Barbarica* of AD 367 may have affected Bath, since there was easy access from the sea and the River Avon at Sea Mills, but nothing has yet come to light to suggest that Irish raiders used this route and came to sack Bath. The town may already have been derelict. There are signs that some people probably clung on into the later fourth century. Dwellings were occupied but eventually fell down and remained in heaps where they had collapsed. The significance is that no-one came as squatters among the debris and no-one picked over the remains for usable building materials. In one of the houses, an oven had been installed in a hole in the floor, and then when it had filled up with ash a new floor and a new oven had been made. When or after the building was abandoned, someone murdered a young girl and threw her head into the oven.[5] No-one came to find the body, reunite it with the head and give the remains a proper burial. In the centre of the town, the temple of Sulis Minerva had fallen down and the baths had started to crumble. Over the heaps of stones and rubble the faithful hot springs bubbled out as they always had, but there was no-one to clear out the mud. Eventually the Roman remains were completely buried, and the surrounding area reverted to marshland around the hot springs, just as it had been in the Iron Age.

After Rome

From the end of the Roman era to the later sixth century nothing is known of Bath. The first documentary evidence is a brief entry in the *Anglo-Saxon Chronicle* concerning the West Saxon kings. In AD 577 King Cealwin won a battle against the Britons at a place called Deorham, which is generally agreed to be Dyrham, a short distance to the north of Bath. The *Chronicle* records that Cealwin defeated three British kings, Coinmail, Condidan and Farinmail, and by doing so he gained control of Gleawanceaster, Cirenceaster, and Bathanceaster, in other words Gloucester, Cirencester and Bath.

If the three British kings are listed in the same order as the towns, then Gloucester and Bath were ruled by the Celtic Coinmail and Farinmail, while Cirencester's king was Condidan, whose name was possibly derived from the Roman Candidianus. The area around these three towns was the domain of the Britons, the greatest centre of their power and influence, and the area has also yielded the greatest concentration of military and civilian metalwork. This small part of the south-west is redolent of lingering Romano-British traditions and government.[6]

The conquest of south-west Britain brought English rule to the western coasts. Cealwin controlled Berkshire, Hampshire, Wiltshire and most of Gloucestershire. But not for much longer.

Fifteen years later in 592, the *Anglo-Saxon Chronicle* records that Cealwin was defeated in a great slaughter and was driven out. By the following year he was dead.

For nearly another century the sources are silent. The fact that the name of the settlement at Bath was recorded by the Anglo-Saxons and was listed amongst the places won by Cealwin shows that a town of some sort existed there, but its size and the number of people living in it are unknown. Its name underwent a few transformations, from Bathanceaster of the *Anglo-Saxon Chronicle* to Akemanceaster, meaning sick man's town, which is related to Akeman Street, leading out of London towards Bath. The Anglo-Saxons obviously appreciated the hot springs, adopting another name for the town, Hoetum Bathum, Hot Bath. The implication is that the springs were still visited and used for cures for aches and pains.[7]

In the seventh century the first religious house was built, presided over by an abbess. The builders may have used some of the Roman stones, many of which were perhaps buried by this time, but the stones of the surviving remains still above ground would have been there for the taking, ready cut and shaped, relieving the builders of the necessity of quarrying stone and transporting it. What pitifully dilapidated state the town would have been in by this time is not known, but in places there may have been some traces of the Roman remains of the baths and the temple still poking through the thick layer of mud that covered the foundations. The Saxon poem called *The Ruin* that is frequently recounted in this connection does not specifically refer to Bath, but it is generally taken to be a description of the town. The poem dates to the eighth century and may have been written by a monk. It refers to buildings erected by giants, collapsed roofs and fallen towers. The author says that all the people have long since disappeared and 100 generations have passed since the buildings were last used. More importantly, he writes of magnificent halls with water flowing through them, and in another passage he refers to courtyards enclosed by stone with a stream gushing forth floods of hot water. If this is not a description of Bath, with neglected buildings crumbling away, but the faithful hot springs still providing gallons of hot water every day, then historians and archaeologists would find it hard to identify another more apt location.

Under King Alfred, Bath features as one of the thirty towns listed in the Burghal Hidage, the document outlining the method of defence against Danish attacks. The document itself was not drawn up until the reign of Alfred's successor Edward the Elder, but the scheme is essentially Alfred's own. The Burghal Hidage lists the number of hides assigned to each defensive centre, the hide being a unit of land measurement. Along with Exeter, Portchester, Winchester and Chichester, among others, Bath was one of the designated defensive centres. These towns possessed walls, mostly Roman in date, though these would be in need of repair by this time and had not always proved successful against attacks.[8]

For the purposes of defence, each hide was to furnish one man and four men were assigned to each pole of the defence works, a stretch of wall measuring about 5 yards. The Burghal Hidage gives no statistics about the size of each town or the length of its defensive circuit, but the number of hides assigned to the towns can be used to calculate the area to be defended. Winchester was Alfred's capital, and it was the largest town, with 2,400 hides. Only Wallingford, guarding a crossing point of the Thames, approached the size of Winchester and possessed the same number of hides. For Winchester, the 2,400 hides would provide 2,400 men, which when divided into groups of four men allows for 600 poles, or a circuit of 3,300 yards. Winchester's medieval walls measured 3,280 yards, so the calculations fit the bill very neatly.[9] Bath was much smaller and would require a smaller number of men for its defence. The relative sizes of Bath and the other towns still reflect the situation of the Roman period.

The Coronation of King Edgar

One of the most important events in the history of Bath was the Coronation of King Edgar of England in 973. By the second half of the tenth century the Danish threat had begun to diminish, and there was a prolonged period of peaceful development with no disruptions from invasions and little internal upheaval. The problem of the northern border was temporarily solved when King Edgar of England met with Kenneth of Scotland and ceded to him all the land between the River Tweed and the River Forth. This is where the border runs nowadays, with the exception of Berwick-upon-Tweed to the north of the river, but between Edgar's reign and the present day much blood has been spilt before the border line was established.

Edgar had succeeded to the throne as a teenager in 959, but he was not formally crowned until 973. Perhaps it was because he waited until total peace reigned that he delayed his Coronation for fourteen years. When the time came, he and the Archbishop of Canterbury, Dunstan, later Saint Dunstan, looked around for a suitable place to hold the Coronation ceremony and chose

Bath. The most important feature of the Coronation was not the actual crowning, but the anointing, and the Church was accorded great prominence in the proceedings. Before Edgar's time there had been no formal procedure or specific order of events for the Coronation of Kings of England. The Coronation at Bath laid down the foundations for all future Coronations up to the present day.

King Edgar entered the church wearing his crown but removed it when the procession approached the high altar, where he prostrated himself. Dunstan led the singing of the *Te Deum*, and then asked the king a series of questions. Edgar's replies to these questions formed the Coronation oath. The king promised to preserve the peace of the kingdom, that robberies and other crimes should be forbidden, and that mercy should qualify and temper all judgements. For the first time, the sovereign acknowledged his obligations to his subjects, rather than demanding an oath of loyalty from them.

It is not certain why Edgar should have chosen Bath as the venue for the Coronation, as opposed to the larger town of Winchester, which in the past had been Alfred's capital and in the future would be the scene for the Coronation of Edward the Confessor. It would also house the treasury of the Norman kings. There were other places besides Winchester where kings were crowned, including Oxford, London and Kingston upon Thames. In 973, Bath clearly possessed some advantage over these other places, and it was probably the church, the predecessor of Bath Abbey.[10] This church, a Benedictine foundation, was quite new in 973, having been built in the middle of the tenth century. Nothing remains of the Saxon work to prove that the church exceeded anything that Winchester, Wells, of Glastonbury could offer, but it must have satisfied Dunstan that it was a suitably prestigious location and had the capacity to hold large numbers of people.

The next documentary evidence for Bath dates from over a century later, when the Domesday Book was compiled and produced in 1086. This was twenty years after the Norman invasion, by which time all the land had been divided up among the barons and minor aristocracy who surrounded William I. The king himself held Bath, with sixty-four burgesses paying £4, and ninety other burgesses of other men paying sixty shillings. There were six waste houses. The Bishop of Coutances held Bathwick, with three ploughs, one villein, ten bordars and two mills. The precise status of bordars is debatable. The bishop also held High Littleton, and in the town of Bath, one burgess paying fifteen pence. Edward of Salisbury held two houses in Bath, rendering seven and a half pence, and Ernulf de Hesdin held three houses in the town, rendering twenty-seven pence. Landholding and rents in Bath were clearly split up between several landowners. The church of Bath held extensive lands around the town, and these brought in considerable sums for the ecclesiastical authorities.

The population of late-eleventh-century Bath was not vast, and in the year after the Domesday Survey was completed it probably dropped considerably. William the Conqueror was dead, and his half-brother, Bishop Odo of Bayeux, fomented rebellion against King William II, or Rufus as he was called. There was no co-ordinated uprising, but sporadic outbreaks of violence. The Bishop of Coutances and his nephew Robert de Mowbray rampaged through Somerset and Wiltshire and burnt Bath. When the rebellion was quelled, Rufus gave the town to Bishop John of Tours, who was responsible for building the Norman Romanesque church that replaced the Saxon version, which had probably been destroyed. In the fifteenth century, when the present abbey was being built, parts of this Norman church were still standing.

By 1100, all trace of the remains of Roman buildings in Bath had probably been obliterated. In that year or thereabouts, the King's Bath was built, and named for King Henry I. It was situated directly above the sacred spring, where a retaining wall had been erected by the first-century Romans, and then later it had been completely enclosed inside a building with a vaulted roof. This roof had fallen in on top of the reservoir and the outlet of the hot spring, which found its way through the debris and then slowly but inexorably brought up mud and silt that eventually buried the Roman features. The mud and silt had built up to such an immense depth that the medieval builders of the King's Bath had no inkling that underneath their establishment there was a much older Roman structure. In the late nineteenth century when the city engineer, Major Davis, was trying to stop a leakage from the King's Bath, the Roman reservoir around the spring was discovered, but it was quickly built over again to provide the renewed floor of the King's Bath. The reservoir remained concealed until excavations were made possible in 1979.

The Legend of King Bladud

It was in the twelfth century that the legend was born of Bladud and the story of how he founded Bath. Statues and images of the mythical Bladud have become a long-standing feature of Bath. His fictional portrait can still be seen in a niche in the King's Bath. The story first appeared in the account of Geoffrey of Monmouth, purporting to be a history of the kings of Britain, *Historia Regum*

Britanniarum, published around 1135. The work is full of fabulous tales, which Geoffrey claimed he had found in another book from Brittany. This may be true as regards this other book, but the stories he recounts do tend to stretch the credulity more than a little. For instance he tells the tale of Merlin fetching the stones of Stonehenge from Ireland, and the first illustrated version of the book, produced many years after it was first written, shows Merlin casually popping one of the lintels on top of two upright stones.

According to Geoffrey, Bladud was heir to the throne of Britain, but on one of his foreign travels he contracted leprosy, and therefore had to give up his claim to be the next king. He retired to a remote farm near Bath, where he became a swineherd. His pigs suffered from sores on their skin, but one day after they had wallowed in the mud of the hot springs, they were miraculously cured, so putting two and two together, Bladud decided to try the hot springs himself, and was also cured. So he went home, became king in his turn and then he built Bath. This was in the eighth century BC, according to Geoffrey of Monmouth, but when he wrote his book he could not have known about what modern historians call the Iron Age. What is more interesting is that he did not know that the Romans had founded Bath, or that underneath the accumulation of mud there was a vast bathing establishment and a temple with a large precinct.

Bath Before the Archaeologists

The first hospitals at Bath were established in the twelfth century, assisting people to use the healing waters of the springs. The numbers of residents and visitors probably did not approach the volume of traffic of the Roman period. The history of Bath for many centuries was predominantly ecclesiastical history, rather than a progressive civic development. By 1230 the town had a mayor, but the poll tax records of 1377 show that the resident population numbered only about 1,000 people.[11] After this documentary evidence there is silence for another 100 years.

At the end of the fifteenth century Bishop Oliver King had his famous dream of angels ascending ladders to heaven, as portrayed on the west front of the abbey. Bishop King started to build the new abbey in 1499, but a mere forty years later, before the old Norman church had been demolished, came the Dissolution of the Monasteries. The future of the abbey looked bleak. Unlike the inhabitants of Tewkesbury, who purchased their abbey and converted it into the parish church, the inhabitants of Bath did not want theirs.

The careful account of Bath made by John Leland is invaluable for its attention to detail. A staunch adherent of Henry VIII, Leland had spent some years listing the contents of monastic libraries, but in the later 1530s and early 1540s he travelled around England noting the various antiquities and points of interest. He compiled copious notes about his travels and in 1545 he settled down to write them all up into book form, ready for publishing. But not long afterwards he had a breakdown and was declared insane. He died, with no book of Itineraries to his name, on 18 April 1552. His work was edited and published later, and there is a version in modern English edited by John Chandler.

Leland visited Bath in 1542. He approached from the south, noting the good meadow lands to the south-west, and the hills which surrounded the valley. He described the several springs from these hills providing water for the town via lead pipes, a product of the lead industry nearby. He also noted that from inside the town the walls were of no great height, but viewed from ground level outside they were much higher. The baths of Leland's time were the Cross Bath, where people suffering from skin complaints visited, and the Hot Bath, much smaller than the Cross Bath. Nearby was St John's Hospital, positioned by Bishop Reginald so as to assist the people using the two baths. The largest bath was the King's Bath, surrounded by an arcade of thirty-two niches where men and women could stand, enjoying some privacy.

Leland devoted considerable attention to the ancient carved stones that he saw, built into the walls and gates. He described them in detail, putting names to them deduced from their attributes; for instance, a figure holding a snake in each hand was probably Hercules. One of the stones showed an infantryman brandishing a sword, and another depicted a running greyhound, with Roman letters inscribed near the dog's tail, but unfortunately Leland could not make sense of what they meant. On another stone he could make out the words meaning 'lived for thirty years'. He doubted that the stones had been placed in the walls during the Roman occupation of Britain, preferring the explanation that they had been gathered up from the remains in the town and used to rebuild the walls.[12] It was clear in the sixteenth century that the Romans had lived in the town, but there was nothing to show that the three separate baths also had Roman origins. The significance of the shortened height of the walls from inside the town is that it probably reveals the depth of the soil covering the Roman remains.

When Elizabeth I visited Bath in 1547, she recommended that the building of abbey should be completed. Work proceeded only very slowly, aided by William Cecil, Lord Burghley, who came to take the waters in 1592. Burghley's steward was Thomas Bellott, a native of Bath and founder of an almshouse in the town. It was probably owing to his influence that Lord Burghley took an interest in the completion of Bath Abbey.

In the seventeenth century, royal patronage of the spa town began to increase. James I visited with his queen, Anne of Denmark, for whom the Queen's Baths were named. Charles II and Queen Catherine arrived in 1663, and in 1687 James II and Queen Mary of Modena took the waters. Around the same time, the much-travelled Celia Fiennes made 'another journey to Bath'. She described how patrons could walk through the water of the King's Baths, holding on to rings at the sides, because the strength of the water could knock people off balance, and it bubbled up very hot 'against the bottoms of one's feet'. The water would turn everything yellow, so canvas bathing suits were worn that were not so affected by the colour. Celia goes on to describe how the baths were emptied around ten or eleven o'clock in the morning after the company left, and then allowed to fill up again ready for the people to bathe in the evening. If anyone did so, the baths were drained again and refilled for morning, but there was such a white scum on the surface that the 'guides' had to skim it off before bathers could use the baths, otherwise they broke out in 'heat and pimples'.[13] The details of how the baths were operated in 1687 gives some idea of how the Romans might have managed the waters.

It was the patronage of Queen Anne, who suffered from gout, that ensured the development of Bath as the foremost spa town in England. She visited in 1702 and 1703, and two years after her last visit there arrived in Bath a young Welshman called Richard

Nash, who as Beau Nash was to dominate and shape Bath society for the next half-century. Nash was born in Carmarthen in 1674 and graduated from Oxford in 1692. He earned most of his income from gambling, so he was nothing if not an adventurer. He founded the Assembly Rooms and moulded the society of Bath in etiquette, behaviour and dress. In 1740 laws were passed to curtail gambling, but Nash circumvented the law by inventing new games. Eventually he fell from favour, and was pensioned off, but not before he had assisted in founding the Mineral Water Hospital.

The facilities offered to visitors in Bath were inadequate for the increasing numbers of people who came to take the waters. The first Pump Room was built in 1706, so the baths were improved, but accommodation for visitors fell far short of the style to which they wished to become accustomed. Housing and accommodation were upgraded when the two architects, John Wood father and son, began to transform the town into the Palladian gem that it is today. Then the infrastructure that supported the bathing establishments had to be improved. More and better drains and sewers were demanded, and it was when a sewer was being constructed along Stall Street in 1727 that the gilt-bronze head of Minerva was discovered, the first and arguably one of the most fantastic finds of the Roman period from the town.

During the eighteenth century, archaeological investigations were conducted with the primary aim of locating and extracting such finds. Marvellous artefacts were considered more important than a study of the remains of buildings, which after all consisted of truncated and decaying walls buried in the ground and barely intelligible compared to the monuments of Greece and Rome that were still standing on the Continent. Knowledge of the Romans in Bath was reliant upon the snippets to be gleaned from ancient literature, and the sculptures and inscriptions that emerged when foundations were being dug for new buildings. Records of what could be seen in the ground along with the finds were only very rarely kept and occasionally it was not even known where exactly the finds came from. There were valuable exceptions. When the foundations were being dug for the Duke of Kingston's baths in 1755, the eastern baths of the Roman complex were revealed and the curved apses with their mosaic floors and hypocausts were beautifully and very clearly drawn.[14] The presence of the temple of Sulis Minerva was first revealed in 1790 when the Pump Room was being extended and rebuilt. The gilt-bronze head of Minerva found in 1727, combined with the inscriptions to the goddess Sulis Minerva, provided more than a few clues to the existence of the temple, but nothing had yet established its whereabouts. It was thought more likely that it was buried underneath the abbey. When more than seventy carved stones emerged from the foundations of the Pump Room, including the Gorgon's head and part of the carved roundel surrounding it, this stupendous series of finds made it clear that the temple was located nearby, and it once stood to the west of the abbey, not underneath it. One stone bears the letters 'VM', probably forming the end of the word 'Templum', but no other finds have yet corroborated the theory.

The podium of the temple was investigated in 1867 and 1868 by James Irvine, who was clerk of works to Sir Gilbert Scott while the restoration of the abbey was in progress. James Irvine reasoned that the temple stretched underneath the cellars of the White Hart Inn and took advantage of the opportunity to investigate when the inn was demolished and new building work was planned. Irvine was meticulous in recording what he saw, and although he left Bath in 1871 he had influenced his friend Richard Mann, who was a builder. Mann was able to make similarly detailed drawings of future excavations when he was employed by the city engineer, Major Charles Davis. One of his first tasks was to dig out the Roman drain running towards the King's Bath, where a leak had started but could not be traced.[15] In the 1870s and 1880s very little was known of the Roman bathing establishment, except for the parts of the eastern bath suite that had been exposed when the Duke of Kingston's baths were built. Cunliffe shows on a plan[16] how various short stretches of walls had been discovered by the nineteenth century, an apsidal section here and a straight section there, but there were not enough connecting sections to be able to make an informed guess as to the appearance of the entire complex. The great gap between the eastern and western parts of the baths could well have meant that there were actually two separate structures. In 1878, two events aided progress. The spring was discovered, labelled the reservoir, and Richard Mann drew it in longitudinal and transverse sections, and in elevation.[17] The dig failed to reach the votive deposits in the mud of the spring before Major Davis laid a floor, supported on concrete pillars, for a new building to be erected over the reservoir. This is how it remained for nearly another century. The reservoir had to wait until the excavations of 1979 for the work to start again, and then the votive offerings were found and put on display in the Roman Baths Museum.

The second event was the purchase by the city council of the buildings around the area of what would be revealed as the Great Bath, to enable Major Davis to dig it. The full extent of the Roman bathing establishment was soon revealed. From 1883 to 1885 the western end of the baths was investigated, and the Circular Bath was consolidated and preserved, and suggestions for building over it successfully foiled. Then the virulent protests about Major Davis's work began, because it was thought that he was destroying much of the evidence for Roman work. In the event, the criticism was not justified, as the excavators of 1979 onwards discovered. Davis was city engineer and had a schedule of new buildings to implement, and far from destroying Roman work, it was found that he had carefully preserved it while erecting new buildings, so there was still an enormous amount of information for modern archaeologists to study once the more recent buildings could be disentangled from the Roman parts.

The creation of the Great Bath as seen today belongs to the Victorian era. It was, and still is, the most spectacular discovery and when fully excavated it deserved to be put on show and used. The temple of Sulis Minerva was not so well known because it could not be excavated in its entirety, parts of it only coming to light in fits and starts. When the Pump Room was extended in 1893, excavation work could be done in the cellars. Major Davis reached Roman floor levels and discovered the entrance to the temple precinct, but it was impossible to be certain about what exactly had been found. Excavating in cellars is not ideal, with all the attendant problems of air quality, inadequate lighting and damp if not wet knees. Archaeologists in Bath must frequently wish for a single period Roman site in an untouched field with natural drainage.

The Duke of Kingston's baths were demolished in 1923, revealing more of the eastern end of the Roman baths, and the appropriately named 1923 bath. This time the work was done and recorded by W. H. Knowles, an experienced archaeologist, who not only recorded what he had found but also published the results. In 1954, Sir Ian Richmond was asked to look at the eastern end of the baths, to try to find the best way of presenting them to the public. After a few archaeological investigations of his own, he was able to make sense of the remains and give an account of the chronology of the baths. Nine years later, in 1963 the Bath Excavation Committee was formed, with Professor Barry Cunliffe at its head. The Bath Archaeological Trust now continues the task. Work began on the temple, first collating all earlier investigations and then starting to dig. The steps up to the temple were discovered in 1964 and the precinct, covered in Roman debris, in the following year.

Plans to excavate underneath the Pump Room in 1978 were put on hold when the waters of the springs were found to be contaminated. Instead, attention was turned to the reservoir covered over by Major Davis's floor supported on concrete pillars. This task lasted until 1983 and many finds from the spring resulted from it. In the following years the western colonnade of the temple precinct was investigated, and in 1994–95 engineering work in York Street provided an opportunity to study the eastern end of the baths again. The full plan of the bathing complex is still not known because there are few opportunities to dig unless buildings are to be demolished, and since many of the buildings in Bath are themselves historically important, further excavation of Roman levels is likely to be sporadic to say the least. Any visitors to Bath with a sense of history, while exploring the town and looking ahead and upwards, reading the blue plaques and trying to get good camera shots of the streets and individual buildings, must surely pause now and then to wonder what other hidden buildings they are walking over at that very moment.

NOTES

1 Bath Before the Romans

1. Aldhouse-Green 2004, 206–8.
2. *RIB* 635.
3. Cunliffe 2000, 12.
4. Woodward 1992, 21–3 fig. 10; 35–6 figs 20; 21; 22; de la Bédoyere 2001, 176 and fig. 128 for reconstruction.
5. Woodward 1992, 21; 24 and fig. 11 plan; de la Bédoyere 2001, 180 and fig. 132 for reconstruction.
6. Woodward 1992, 66; de la Bédoyere 2010, 242–3; Aldhouse-Green 2004, 200–1.

2 The Romans Arrive

1. Strabo 4.5.3.
2. Dio 49.38.2; 53.22.5; 53.25.2.
3. *Res Gestae* 32.
4. Suetonius *Lives of the Caesars*, Caligula 44.2.
5. Dio 50.19.1.
6. *RIB* II 2404.1.
7. *RIB* II 2404.2.
8. Cunliffe 2000, 13.
9. Cunliffe and Devonport 1985, 9.
10. *RIB* I 158.
11. Hassall 2000, 63.
12. *RIB* II 2404.3.
13. *RIB* II 2404.38.
14. Wacher 1974, 256.
15. Cunliffe 1998, 107.
16. *RIB* I 92.
17. Wacher 1974, 257; 280.
18. Wilson 2002, 112.
19. Cunliffe 1971, 23–4.
20. Tacitus *Agricola* 14.
21. *RIB* I 91.
22. Bogaers, 1979.

3 Bath Begins

1. Suetonius *Lives of the Caesars*, Nero 18.

2. Birley 2005, 42 says that this idea was suggested at the time of the disaster, then when Paullinus had won the final victory, the policy was changed and it was decided to keep control of Britain.
3. Tacitus *Annals*, 14.33.
4. Wacher 1974, 41.
5. Wacher 1974, 18.
6. Millett, 1990.
7. *RIB* I 172.
8. Ptolemy *Geography*, 2.3.13.
9. Wacher 1974, 436 no. 49, quoting a comment by A. L. F. Rivet.
10. *RIB* I 145.
11. Tacitus *Agricola*, 14.
12. Cunliffe 1971, 71–127; 1998, 49–90.
13. *RIB* I 91.
14. Birley 2005, 467–8.
15. Birley 2005, 468 no. 13 quoting Rivet and Smith 1979, 445–6.
16. Wilson 2002, 111–2.
17. Millett 1990, 68; Haselgrove 1984, 34–5.
18. De la Bédoyere 2006, 135.
19. Rivet 1968, 51.
20. Salway 1991, 93 no. 2.
21. *RIB* I 151.
22. *RIB* I 105.
23. Cunliffe 2000, 53.
24. Pliny *Natural History*, 34.164.
25. Cunliffe 2000, 89.
26. Hodge 2002, 264.
27. De la Bédoyere 2001, 31.
28. Tacitus *Annals*, 14.31–2.
29. De la Bédoyere 2001, 269 fig. 122.
30. *RIB* I 91.
31. Cunliffe 2000, 41–4.
32. Cunliffe 2000, 40.
33. Cunliffe 2000, 43–5.
34. De la Bédoyere 2001, 171; 172 figs 124, 125, for both styles in

reconstruction drawings.
35. Cunliffe 2000, 46.

4 Bath Flourishes

1. *RIB* I 146.
2. *RIB* I 150
3. *RIB* I 138
4. *RIB* I 153.
5. Cunliffe 2000, 115.
6. Wacher 1974, 375–410.
7. Wilson 2002, 116–7.
8. Wilson 2002, 177; the rebuilding was necessitated because the basilica had been built over the filled-in ditches of the fort and had begun to subside.
9. Wacher 1974, 360–2.
10. *RIB* I 288.
11. Bennett 2001, 15–6.
12. *Historia Augusta* Hadrian 18.
13. *Historia Augusta* Hadrian 22
14. Rook 2002, 18; Carcopino 1956, 257–325.
15. Cunliffe 2000, 89–95 for the first series of alterations to the baths.
16. Carcopino 1956, 257–325; an inscription from the baths at the mining town of Vipasca in Lusitania (*CIL* II 5181) reveals that women bathed from the first hour to the end of the seventh hour, and the men from the beginning of the eighth hour to the end of the second hour of the night.
17. Cunliffe 2000, 94 says that the evidence allows the alterations to have taken place in Hadrian's reign.
18. Cunliffe 2000, 90.
19. Cunliffe 2000, 93.
20. Cunliffe 2000, 91.
21. Cunliffe 2000, 95–104.
22. Cunliffe 2000, 45–6.
23. Cunliffe 2000, 46 fig. 24.
24. Cunliffe 2000, fig. 37 for reconstruction drawing; de la Bédoyere 2001, plate 24.
25. For reconstruction drawings see Cunliffe 2000, 59 fig. 37; de la Bédoyere 2001, 172–3 figs 125–6.
26. *CSIR* 1.2, 28.

27. *CSIR* 1.2, 52 and 53.
28. Cunliffe 2000, 59–60.
29. *CSIR* 1.2, 21–3.
30. *CSIR* 1.2, 4–19; Cunliffe 2000, 65 fig. 42.
31. *RIB* I 141.
32. Cunliffe 2000, 67 fig. 43.
33. Cunliffe 2000, 112.
34. Cunliffe 2000, 110–2 figs 81–2.
35. Cunliffe 2000, 121–2.
36. *RIB* I 145.
37. Cunliffe 2000, 117.
38. Cunliffe 2000, 118–20.
39. Aldhouse-Green 2004, 200–6
40. *CSIR* 1.2. no. 25; Cunliffe 2000, 70 fig. 47a.
41. De la Bédoyere 2006, 158 labels the head as Oceanus; Wilson 2002, 161, says that the identification is to be dismissed; see Stewart 1981, 47–55 on the Gorgon's head and the relationship to Medusa.
42. Stewart 1981, 80–1 argues that the supposed root word *Sul* is not cognate with Latin *Sol*; Rivet and Smith 1979, 256 point out that the nominative form is *Sulis* not *Sul*, as was once thought, and there is no connection with Celtic words for the sun.
43. Alcock 2006, 74 fig. 31.
44. Aldhouse-Green 2004, 201.
45. Cunliffe 2000, 46–50, figs 25a and 25b.
46. *RIB* I 138.
47. Cunliffe 2000, 68 fig. 45.
48. Cunliffe 1988, no. 97.
49. *RIB* I 140.
50. Aldhouse-Green 2004, 205.
51. *CSIR* 1.2 39; Cunliffe 2000, 71 fig. 47b.
52. *RIB* I 151.
53. *RIB* I 192.
54. *RIB* I 105.
55. *RIB* I 106.
56. *RIB* I 1035.
57. *RIB* I 159.
58. *CSIR* 1.2.44.
59. *RIB* I 139.
60. *RIB* I 146.
61. *RIB* I 152.

62. *RIB* I 1041.
63. For the curse tablets from Bath see Tomlin 1988.
64. Woodward 1992, 71–3 figs 56–7.
65. Wild 2004, 302.
66. *RIB* I 154.
67. De la Bédoyere 2006, 223.

5 Bath People

1. *RIB* I 140.
2. *RIB* I 155.
3. Cunliffe 2000, 33–4 fig. 12; 49–50.
4. Solinus *Collectanea Rerum Memorabilium*, 22.10.
5. Salway 1991, 631; Cunliffe 2000, 24.
6. Cunliffe 2000, 49.
7. On the use of public baths and how they were run see Balsdon 1969, 26–32; Carcopino 1956, 253–62; Paoli 1963, 221–7. The older books are still useful because they contain numerous references to ancient literature and inscriptions.
8. Paoli 1963, 222.
9. Balsdon 1969, 28; *ILS* 5686.
10. Paoli 1963, 222–3.
11. *ILS* 5795.
12. Tacitus *Agricola*, 21.
13. De la Bédoyere 2006, 158.
14. *RIB* I 149.
15. *RIB* I 151.
16. *RIB* I 105.
17. Cunliffe 2000, 117–8.
18. Balsdon 1969, 29, 359 no. 69.
19. Balsdon 1969, 360 no. 72.
20. Cunliffe 2000, 134–5.
21. *RIB* I 138.
22. *RIB* I 143.
23. *RIB* I 144.
24. De la Bédoyere 2006, 223.
25. *RIB* I 155.
26. *RIB* I 163.
27. *RIB* I 165.
28. *RIB* I 164.
29. *RIB* I 162.
30. *RIB* I 160.
31. *RIB* I 158.
32. *RIB* I 156.
33. *RIB* I 157.

34. Seneca *Epistles*, 56.1–2.
35. Cunliffe 2000, 123–5.
36. Cunliffe 2000, 125.
37. Cunliffe 2000, 106–27; de la Bédoyere 2006, 158–9.
38. Cunliffe 2000, 127.
39. *RIB* I 161.
40. *RIB* I 141; Cunliffe 2000, 67; 128.
41. *RIB* I 152.
42. *RIB* I 587.
43. *RIB* I 583.

6 Bath Declines & Revives

1. *RIB* I 1427.
2. *RIB* I 103.
3. Ammianus Marcellinus 18.2.3–4; Zosimus 3.5.2.
4. Cunliffe 2000, 104–5.
5. Cunliffe 2000, 120.
6. Myres 1986, 169.
7. Blair 1977, 35.
8. Stenton 1971, 264–5.
9. Blair 1977, 293–4.
10. Little 1980, 12–3.
11. Little 1980, 18.
12. Chandler 1993, 407.
13. Morris 1982, 45–7.
14. Cunliffe 2000. 73 fig. 48.
15. Cunliffe 2000, 29–30.
16. Cunliffe 2000, 75 fig. 49.
17. Cunliffe 2000, 31 fig. 11.

Abbreviations

CIL *Corpus Inscriptionum Latinarum* (1863 onwards).

CSIR *Corpus Signorum Imperii Romani: Great Britain*, Vol. 1 Fascicule 2 Bath and the Rest of Wessex (Oxford University Press for British Academy, 1982).

ILS *Inscriptiones Latinae Selectae* (ed. H. Dessau) (2nd ed., 3 vols, Berlin: 1954–5).

RIB Roman Inscriptions in Britain, Vol. 1 *Inscriptions on Stone* (1965, 1995), *Vol. 2 Instrumentum Domesticum, Fascicules 1 to 8* (1990–5).

BIBLIOGRAPHY &
FURTHER READING

Ancient Works

Caesar, *Gallic War* (Loeb).
Dio, *Roman History* (Loeb).
Pliny, *Natural History* (Loeb).
Ptolemy, *Geography*.
Strabo, *Geography* (Loeb).
Suetonius, *Lives of the Caesars* (Loeb).
Tacitus, *Agricola* (Loeb).
Tacitus, *Annals* (Loeb).
Tacitus, *Histories* (Loeb).

Modern Works

Alcock, J. P., *Life in Roman Britain* (History Press, 2010).
Aldhouse-Green, M., 'Gallo-British Deities and Their Shrines' in Todd, M. (ed.), *A Companion to Roman Britain* (Blackwell, 2004) pp. 193–219.
Balsdon, J. P. V. D., *Life and Leisure in Ancient Rome* (Bodley Head, 1969).
Bennett, J., *Towns in Roman Britain* (3rd ed., Shire, 2001).
Birley, A. R., *The People of Roman Britain* (Batsford, 1979, reprinted 1988).
Birley, A. R., *The Roman Government of Britain* (Oxford University Press, 2005).
Blagg, T. F. C. and A. C. King, *Military and Civilian in Roman Britain* (Oxford: 1984).
Blair, P. H. *An Introduction to Anglo-Saxon England* (2nd ed., Cambridge University Press, 1977).
Bogaers, J. E., 'King Cogidubnus in Chichester: Another Reading of *RIB* 91', *Britannia*, 10 (1979) pp. 243–54.
Boon, G. C., *Silchester: The Roman Town of Calleva* (David and Charles, 1974).
Brewer, R. J. (ed.), *Roman Fortresses and Their Legions* (Society of Antiquaries of London and National Museums and Galleries of Wales, 2000).
Burnham, B. C. and J. Wacher, *The 'Small Towns' of Roman Britain* (Batsford, 1990).
Carcopino, J., *Daily Life in Ancient Rome* (Pelican Books, 1956).

Chandler, J. (ed.), *John Leland's Itinerary: Travels in Tudor England* (Alan Sutton Publishing, 1993).

Collingwood, R. G. and R. P. Wright, *Roman Inscriptions of Britain, Vol. 1 Inscriptions on Stone* (Rev. ed. R. S. O. Tomlin with addenda and corrections, Alan Sutton Publishing, 1995).

Collingwood, R. G. and R. P. Wright, *Roman Inscriptions of Britain, Vol. 2 Instrumentum Domesticum* (Rev. ed. S. S. Frere and R. S. O. Tomlin, Alan Sutton Publishing, 1990–5).

Croom, A. T., *Roman Clothing and Fashion* (History Press, 2000).

Crummy, P. J., *City of Victory: The Story of Colchester, Britain's First Roman Town* (Colchester: 1997).

Cunliffe, B., *Fishbourne: A Roman Palace and Its Garden* (Thames and Hudson, 1971).

Cunliffe, B., 'The Temple of Sulis Minerva at Bath. Vol. 2: The Finds from the Sacred Spring', *Oxford University Committee for Archaeology*, 16 (1988).

Cunliffe, B., *Fishbourne Roman Palace* (Tempus Publishing, 1998).

Cunliffe, B., *Roman Bath Discovered* (History Press, 2000).

Cunliffe, B. and P. Devonport, 'The Temple of Sulis Minerva at Bath. Vol. 1: The Site', *Oxford University Committee for Archaeology*, 7 (1985).

De la Bédoyère, G., *Roman Villas and the Countryside* (Batsford, 1993).

De la Bédoyère, G., *Companion to Roman Britain* (Tempus Publishing, 1999).

De la Bédoyère, G., *Buildings of Roman Britain* (Tempus Publishing, 2001).

De la Bédoyère, G., *Towns of Roman Britain* (Tempus Publishing, 2003).

De la Bédoyère, G., *Roman Britain: A New History* (Thames and Hudson, 2006).

Morris, C. (ed.), *The Illustrated Journeys of Celia Fiennes c. 1682–c. 1712* (Webb and Bower/Michael Joseph, 1982).

Frere, S. S., *Britannia: A History of Roman Britain* (3rd ed., Pimlico, 1987).

Haselgrove, C. C., 'Romanization Before the Conquest: Gaulish Precedents and British Consequences' in Blagg and King (eds), *Military and Civilian in Roman Britain* (Oxford: 1984) pp. 1–64.

Hassall, M., 'Pre-Hadrianic Legionary Dispositions in Britain' in Brewer, R. J. (ed.), *Roman Fortresses and Their Legions* (Society of Antiquaries of London and National Museums and Galleries of Wales, 2000) pp. 51–68.

Henig, M., *Religion in Roman Britain* (Batsford, 1984).

Hodge, A. T., *Roman Aqueducts and Water Supply* (2nd ed., Duckworth, 2002).

Ireland, S., *Roman Britain: A Sourcebook* (Routledge, 1996).

Jones, B. and D. Mattingley, *An Atlas of Roman Britain* (Oxbow Books, 1990).

Lewis, M. J. T., *Temples in Roman Britain* (Cambridge University Press, 1965).

Little, B., *Bath Portrait: The Story of Bath, Its Life and Its Buildings* (The Burleigh Press, 1980).

Liversidge, J., *Britain in the Roman Empire* (Routledge and Kegan Paul, 1968).

Macready. S. and F. H. Thompson (eds), *Cross-Channel Trade Between Gaul and Britain in the Pre-Roman Iron Age* (London: 1984).

Millett, M., *The Romanization of Britain: An Essay in Archaeological Interpretation* (Cambridge University Press, 1990).

Myres, J. N. L., *The English Settlements* (Oxford University Press, 1989).

Percival, J., *The Roman Villa* (Batsford, 1976).

Paoli, U. E., *Rome: Its People, Life and Customs* (Longman, 1965; republished by Bristol Classical Press, 1990).

Rivet, A. L. F., *Town and Country in Roman Britain* (Hutchinson Press, 1968).

Rivet, A. L. F. and C. Smith, *The Place Names of Roman Britain* (Batsford, 1979).

Rodwell, W. (ed.), 'Temples, Churches and Religion in Roman Britain', *British Archaeological Reports, British Series*, 77 (1980).

Rook, T., *Roman Baths in Britain* (Shire, 2002).

Salway, P., *Roman Britain* (Oxford University Press, 1991).

Salway, P., *The Oxford Illustrated History of Roman Britain* (Oxford: 1993).

Smith, J. T., *Roman Villas: A Study in Social Structure* (London, 1997).

Stenton, F., *Anglo-Saxon England* (3rd ed., Oxford University Press, 1971).

Stewart, B., *The Waters of the Gap: The Mythology of Aquae Sulis* (Bath City Council, 1981).

Todd, M. (ed.), *Studies in the Romano-British Villa* (Leicester University Press, 1978).

Todd, M. (ed.), *A Companion to Roman Britain* (Blackwell, 2004).

Tomlin, R. S. O., 'The Curse Tablets' in Cunliffe, B., 'The Temple of Sulis Minerva at Bath. Vol. 2: The Finds from the Sacred Spring', *Oxford University Committee for Archaeology*, 16 (1988) pp. 59–277.

Wacher, J., *The Towns of Roman Britain* (Batsford, 1974).

Wild, J. P., 'Textiles and Dress' in Todd (ed.), *A Companion to Roman Britain* (Blackwell, 2004) pp. 299–308.

Wilson, R. J. A., *A Guide to Roman Remains in Britain* (4th ed., Constable, 2002).

Woodward, A., *Shrines and Sacrifice* (Batsford, 1992).

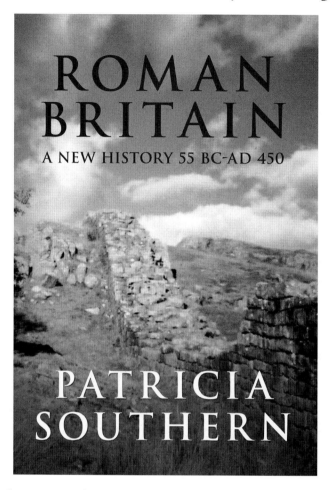

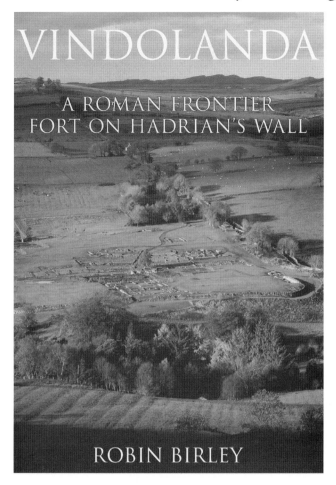

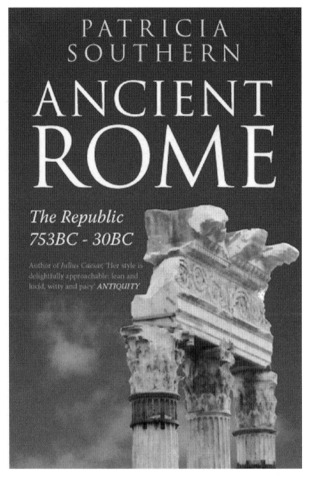

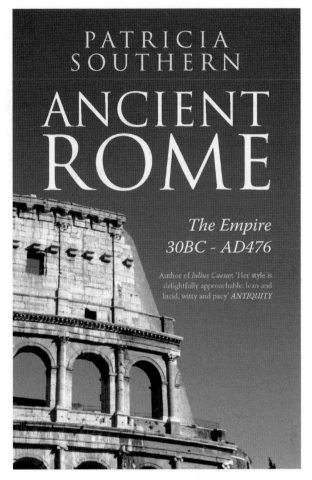

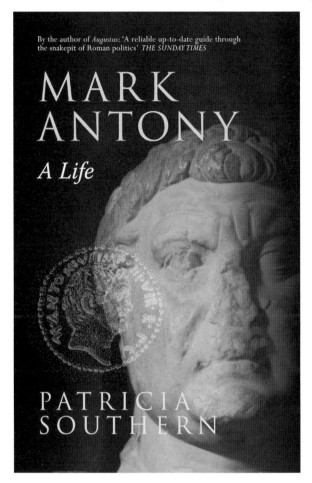

Also available from Amberley Publishing

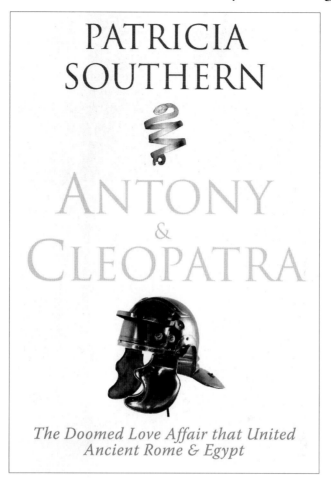

PATRICIA SOUTHERN

ANTONY
&
CLEOPATRA

*The Doomed Love Affair that United
Ancient Rome & Egypt*

The story of one of the most compelling love affairs in history

The immortal lovers of novels, plays and films, Antony and Cleopatra were reviled by contemporary Romans, but history has transformed them into tragic heroes. Somewhere between their vilification by Augustus and the judgement of a later age there were two vibrant people whose destinies were entwined after the assassination of Julius Caesar in March 44 BC. Mark Antony's reputation for recklessness, hard drinking, and womanising overshadowed his talents for leadership and astute administration. Cleopatra was determined to reconstitute the ancient empire of the Ptolemies, and Antony as legally appointed ruler of the east gave her much, but not all, of what she desired.

£9.99 Paperback
38 illustrations
208 pages
978-1-4456-0576-0

Available from all good bookshops or to order direct
Please call **01453–847–800**
www.amberleybooks.com

Also available from Amberley Publishing

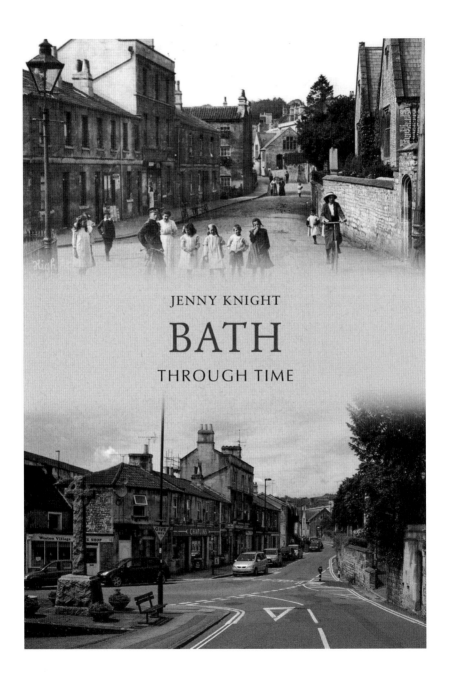

JENNY KNIGHT

BATH

THROUGH TIME

Available from all good bookshops or to order direct
Please call **01453-847-800**
www.amberleybooks.com

Also available from Amberley Publishing

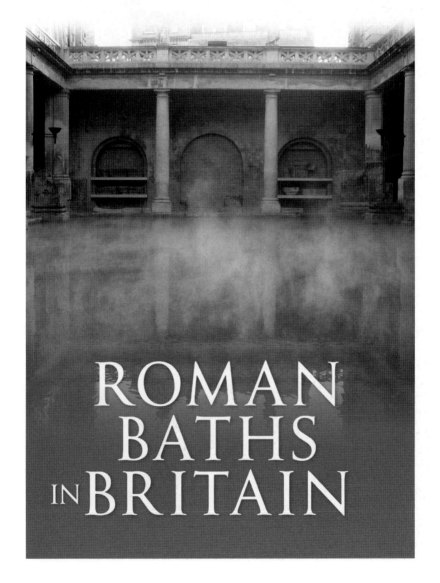

IAN D. ROTHERHAM

ROMAN
BATHS
IN BRITAIN

Available from all good bookshops or to order direct
Please call **01453–847–800**
www.amberleybooks.com

Also available from Amberley Publishing

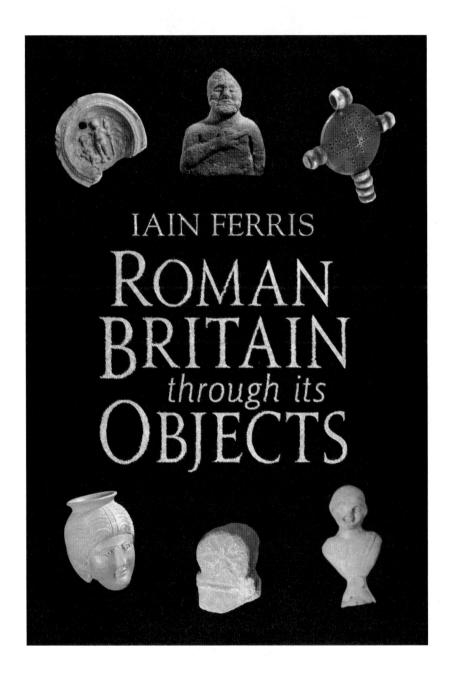

IAIN FERRIS

ROMAN BRITAIN *through its* OBJECTS

Available from all good bookshops or to order direct
Please call **01453-847-800**
www.amberleybooks.com

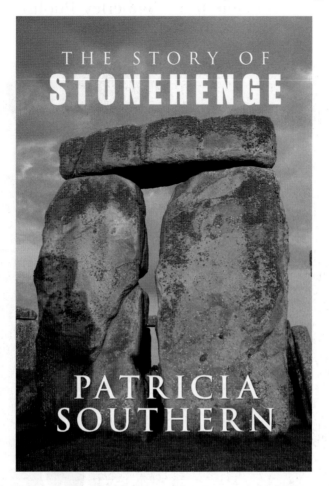

Also available from Amberley Publishing

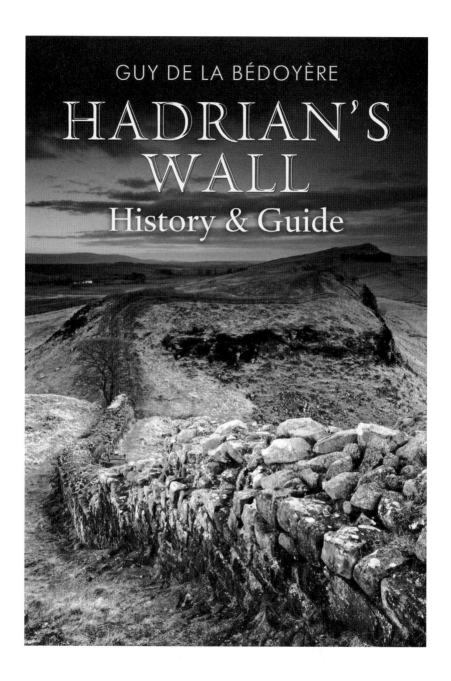

GUY DE LA BÉDOYÈRE

HADRIAN'S WALL
History & Guide

INDEX